Edward Thomas's Poets

EDWARD THOMAS was born in London in 1878 and was educated at Lincoln College, Oxford. He published his first book, a collection of essays on the country, in 1897, with the encouragement of the critic James Ashcroft Noble. In 1899, while he was still an undergraduate, Thomas married Helen Noble (1877-1967), the daughter of his mentor. Their son Mervyn was born in 1900 and their elder daughter Bronwen in 1902. Myfanwy Thomas, their third child, was born in 1910. The family moved house frequently, but from 1906 lived in or near Petersfield, Hampshire. The landscape of the area was to have a strong influence on Thomas's poetry. Thomas sought to make a living as a writer, reviewing and publishing essays, anthologies, biographies, guidebooks and country writing. The strain of reconciling his own creativity with the need to earn enough to support his family created periods of deep depression during these years. From 1901 onwards, Thomas corresponded with a number of writer-friends. Before Petersfield, his main correspondents included Jesse Berridge, Gordon Bottomley and Edward Garnett. He became close to W.H. Davies in 1905, and began friendships with Walter de la Mare and W.H. Hudson in 1906. He began corresponding with Eleanor Farjeon in 1912 and with Robert Frost in 1913. These years coincided with his experiments in fiction and autobiographical writing and the onset of his mature poetry. In 1915 Thomas enlisted in the Artists' Rifles, transferring a year later to the Royal Artillery, where he trained as a map-reading instructor and was commissioned second lieutenant. He volunteered for service overseas and was posted to France in January 1917. On 9 April Thomas was killed at the battle of Arras. Most of his poetry was published posthumously: *Poems* (1917) under his pseudonym, Edward Eastaway, *Last Poems* in 1918 and his *Collected Poems* in 1920.

JUDY KENDALL is a poet and translator. She has a doctorate in the process of poetic composition with reference to Edward Thomas and holds a lectureship in English and Creative Writing at the University of Salford.

Edward Thomas's Poets

edited by Judy Kendall

CARCANET

First published in Great Britain in 2007 by
Carcanet Press Limited
Alliance House
Cross Street
Manchester M2 7AQ

A CIP catalogue record for this book is available from the British Library
ISBN 978 1 85754 908 9

The publisher acknowledges financial assistance from Arts Council England

Typeset by XL Publishing Services, Tiverton
Printed and bound in England by SRP Ltd, Exeter

i.m.
three sisters

Emmie Kendall

Juie Capron

Peg Cole

from the 1890s on, raconteurs all

Contents

EDWARD THOMAS'S POETS

Contents

Contents

Edward Thomas:
Contexts and Correspondences

Edward Thomas, like his poetry, seems to arrive suddenly out of nowhere. There is a persistent image of him, a tall, gaunt, arresting figure, coming into focus out of a kind of Celtic mist, appearing on the scene as unexpectedly as his final two years of poetry pour unstoppably onto the page. And yet this maverick and apparently unlocatable poet, neither Georgian nor Modern, neither Welsh nor English, neither rural nor urban, whose slim brief poetic *oeuvre* comprises only a fraction of his output as a writer, is also distinctive for the far-reaching legacy he has left subsequent poets. He has a reputation with many of them as a model of poetic composition, a 'poet's poet'. W.H. Auden, in reference to his own poem 'Rain', coined the epithet 'Edward Thomasy', and the writing of 'Edward Thomasy' poems has become something of a tradition among writers as diverse as Elizabeth Bartlett, Alison Brackenbury, Gillian Clarke, U.A. Fanthorpe, Seamus Heaney, Ted Hughes, Elizabeth Jennings, Philip Larkin, Alun Lewis, Michael Longley, Tom Paulin, Kathleen Raine, Carole Satyamurti, E.J. Scovell, R.S. Thomas and Derek Walcott.

However true this picture may be, it is pertinent to remember that in his time Thomas was a highly regarded critic of contemporary poetry. Theresa Whistler records in *Imagination of the Heart: The Life of Walter de la Mare* that when, in 1906, the editor Sir Henry Newbolt learnt of Thomas's request to include Walter de la Mare's 'Keep Innocency' in an anthology, he told de la Mare that Thomas's praise was 'worth all the rest' of the London reviewers, and that it was 'a real score to have pleased him'. In 1907, Arthur Ransome wrote a full-length *Bookman* feature on Thomas, celebrating his achievements as critic and country essayist. Thomas was a regular member, along with other writers and artists such as Hilaire Belloc, Muirhead Bone, W.H. Davies, W.H. Hudson, Thomas Seccombe, R.A. Scott-James, Stephen Reynolds, Ford Madox Ford, and occasionally Joseph

Conrad and John Galsworthy, at the publisher's reader Edward Garnett's weekly Soho lunches. Thomas also set up his own London teatime coterie in St Martin's Lane, meeting, among others, the poets W.H. Davies, Walter de la Mare, John Freeman, Ralph Hodgson and Robert Frost. In addition, during his writing career, Thomas kept in close epistolary contact with a number of literary friends: Jesse Berridge, Gordon Bottomley, Walter de la Mare, Eleanor Farjeon, John Freeman, Robert Frost, Edward Garnett, J.W. Haines and W.H. Hudson. The work of many of them appears in Thomas's published books. At times this seems to serve the mundane purpose of making up a commissioned word count by means of an anonymous or attributed quotation, but extracts from their work also appear more formally as epigraphs, translations of Welsh songs and anthology entries, and are less deliberately echoed in a number of Thomas's poems. This incorporation in his writing of the work of other poets is significant. In a letter of 18 March 1915 to Hudson, Thomas stressed the brevity of his poetic career, writing of his poems:

> They have all been written since November. I had done no verses before and did not expect to and merely became nervous when I thought of beginning.

But this poetic turn was not as sudden as Thomas makes it appear. Rather, it was a gradual process arising out of responses to earlier writing. As far back as 1900, Thomas refers to himself as 'a very minor "prose poet"' in a letter to his friend Ian MacAlister, and in a letter to Gordon Bottomley dated 6 August 1904 he talks of writing a 'petite poème en prose'. In 1905, he slips his 'pseudo translation' of a non-existent Welsh lyric 'Eluned' into *Beautiful Wales*, and in 1913, he records an aborted attempt at poetry in a letter to de la Mare written on 7 September 1913 and in an essay, 'Insomnia', published in *The Last Sheaf.*

Thomas's correspondence

The relation between Thomas's poems and his correspondence with close writer friends forms the subject of *Edward Thomas's Poets*. The letters not only set his writings firmly in the context of literary activity of his time but also act as a valuable record of his composing processes. In this voluminous correspondence, now scattered across libraries and repositories in the UK and America, Thomas shares his struggles and experiments in composition with contemporary writers. From 1902 onwards, he is almost continually in the process of conducting discussions of work, theories and creative ideas with one or other of his correspondents, often writing several letters a day, sometimes to the same person. An indication of the frequency of this correspondence occurs in a letter to his wife of 9 October 1914:

> A letter from Mrs Frost. They expect me on Wednesday. So address letters here up to *Monday first post*. I shall leave here early on Tuesday; probably stay Tuesday night at Brecon and reach the Frosts on Wednesday evening unless it's wet, in which case I shall train there on Tuesday, so please send Monday's, Tuesday's, Wednesday's and Thursday's letters to me at the Frosts'.

Thomas fuelled the energy of his literary correspondence with meetings in town, at his and his friends' homes, and on walking tours in the country. In many cases the friendship extended to his friends' families. On 22 September 1907, in a letter to Gordon Bottomley, he addresses his request for help with a new book to Bottomley's wife, as well: 'Does anything occur to you & Emily?' He tested his stories out on his own and his friends' children; he exchanged letters with his friends' wives; and their children visited each other's homes.

It was Thomas's regular practice to send his friends works-in-progress for comments and criticism. Often, in turn, they sent him theirs. The important role these letters played in Thomas's writing projects is indisputable. Thomas and his friends shared ideas, dreams and drafts of prose and poetry, plans for collaborative writing, translating, editing and illustration projects, proofreading details and advice about marketing and publication. Thomas even draws on his letters as direct sources and records of creative ideas, on a number of occasions instructing his wife to file or return letters he has written for later use in his writing, as in his letter to her of 11 February 1913: 'I hope you won't mind if I make this a notebook as well as a letter.'

The high value Thomas placed on letter-writing is discernible in the physicality of his letters. The text is laid out clearly in even and mostly legible handwriting, with an idiosyncratic use of spacing in word divisions and punctuation that appears to reflect the sense, rhythm and emphasis of the text. He takes the physical act of letter-writing seriously, noting to Jesse Berridge on 20 October 1907 that 'a mere half hour wedged in among work doesn't make a letter'. He is concerned with the content and tone, apologising to Gordon Bottomley for a letter full of 'generalities' on 3 September 1914, and to Robert Frost for a detected tone of insincerity on 31 October 1914.

Occasionally, a direct equation between epistolary and creative work occurs, and letters are replaced by poems. On 17 October 1915, Thomas sends Eleanor Farjeon 'October' with the words '[W]ill you take some verses for a letter?'; in early 1915, Frost sent him an envelope including nothing except 'Two Roads', an early version of 'The Road Not Taken'; and in December 1916 Farjeon sends him her poem 'St Mary Axe' as a Christmas card.

Thomas's prose

Before he began to write poetry, Thomas's letters to his literary friends comprise a detailed record of his development as a prose writer, his dissatisfaction with earlier approaches to composition, and his search for more suitable forms and methods. This record acts as an accompaniment to the trajectory of his successive prose books, which track the development of Thomas's style, as succinctly summarised by Edna Longley in *Poems and Last Poems*. In her introduction to the notes, she shows how Thomas's prose works lead to his final poetry, reflecting his constant search for a right way of writing:

> Each successive Nature book by Thomas involved repetition yet was differently organised, which suggests a continual effort to combine the same elements in a clinching form. Every attempt signalled some minor advance. In *The Heart of England* and *The South Country* he laid down his imaginative terrain; in *The Icknield Way* and *In Pursuit of Spring* he established his symbolism of the road or journey (and in the latter of the seasons). Again, the dutifully executed *Celtic Stories* and *Norse Tales* helped to nourish the very individual mythology that emerged in *Four-and-Twenty Blackbirds* and *Lob*. Even a loathed pot-boiler like *A Literary Pilgrim in England* gave Thomas the opportunity to relate literature to landscape more continuously than in any of his other books, and by implication to define his own artistic relation to England. In *The Happy-go-lucky Morgans* and *The Childhood of Edward Thomas* he probed and shaped his past life more intensively than ever before. The books on Jefferies and Borrow led to himself; while the studies of Pater, Swinburne and Maeterlinck confirmed the toppling of youthful idols in a rite of exorcism. Finally, the very fact that Thomas's poems were 'like quintessences of the best parts of my prose books' (letter to John Freeman, Moore, p.326) indicates that there was something to distil.

Edna Longley, though, omits any mention of Thomas's one critical work in which the process of poetic composition forms the main subject: *Feminine Influence on the Poets* (1910). This book is of particular interest in considering the relation of Thomas's letters to his composing processes, since passages from the letters are incorporated as part of its argument. Thomas's research for the book involved asking literary friends for accounts of their processes of composition, and integrating their responses anonymously in the finished work. As a result, in *Feminine Influence*, text drawn from Thomas's correspondence is placed in direct relation to investigations of processes of composition. Although Thomas's assessment of *Feminine Influence* is only mildly favourable, it compares well with his customary vicious denigration of his published prose books, and suggests a greater warmth of interest in the subject-matter – poetic composition. He writes to Gordon Bottomley and Jesse Berridge at the end of 1910 that it is a 'wretched' book and 'shockingly put together', but also stresses that it is 'full of material you may like to have gathered together', and emphasises detail of its composing process, detail that pre-empts later experiments in composition: 'I put down all but everything just as it occurred during the few months I was doing it.'

Thomas's focus on the composing process in *Feminine Influence* and the less direct ways in which, as Edna Longley so cogently elucidates, his other prose works touch on the subject, are augmented by frequent allusions to composing processes in his literary correspondence. This correspondence tracks his movement as a writer from forms that dissatisfy to forms that more nearly meet his requirements, and from a way of writing that splits between an instinctual and a deliberate approach to composition to his discovery and acceptance of an informed instinctive approach. This shows that his later poems are not so much departures from his earlier prose, as a natural progression from them, 'quintessences' of them, as he observed to John Freeman in 1915. Like the prose books and the letters, his poems, almost self-reflexively, touch on processes of composition in their subject matter, style and form.

Thomas's letters express satisfaction and delight in the act of poetic composition and the ease of that act. He observes to Eleanor Farjeon on 25 March 1915 that 'I can sometimes hardly wait to light my fire' before starting to write verses and on 18 March 1915 to W.H. Hudson that 'when it came to beginning I slipped into it naturally whatever the results'. These comments suggest Thomas had reached an apotheosis in his search for right ways to write. Significantly, however, Thomas's poems continue to record and reflect the process of searching for a means of poetic composition within their subject-matter, form and style. Particular examples that present a reflection, and refraction, of Thomas's search for a way of composing are 'Go now', 'Words' and 'Aspens'. In them he learns to be content within the process, and to focus on minute aspects of it, on the 'not knowing' and the 'not arriving', positioned at the cross-roads before a decision is made. Such resolutions take the place of definitive answers to his probings and help to explain his special position as a 'poet's poet'. His poems, which he spent so much of his writing life not writing but working towards, act, in their reflection of the poetic processes from which they originate, almost as a poetic manual on composing. The examination in *Edward Thomas's Poets* of the close relation between the subject of poetic composition and the very fabric of Thomas's mature poetry, which his correspondence helps reveal, allows for new and deep readings of Thomas's poems.

Thomas's composing processes in prose

Thomas's initial difficulties in composition are recorded as early as 21 June 1897: writing from Swindon to Helen Noble, his future wife, he laments his self-consciousness as a writer: 'I even think of how I could describe it [a scene in nature], actually while I gaze! how mean! how ridiculous! what prose fancy!' In his essay for *In Memoriam: Edward Thomas*, J.W. Haines records how Thomas discussed in his last years the difficulties caused him as a writer by his dependence on notebooks in his prose and earlier poems:

> [F]or years, on his walks and rides, he made the most elaborate notes as he went along and afterwards used these for his books and essays. He said he had even done this with some of his earlier Poems; but that he had come to the conclusion that what was really valuable remained in the mind, and that notes were rather a hindrance than a help, because they preserved the memory of unimportant things which would otherwise be forgotten.

However, as a letter of 17 March 1904 to Gordon Bottomley reveals, along with his self-consciousness and his habit of depending on note-books, from early on Thomas also experienced a more instinctual approach to writing:

> I look forward to writing & look back upon it joyfully as if it were

an achievement & not an attempt – very often. But while I write, it is a dull blindfold journey through a strange lovely land: I seem to take what I write from the dictation of someone else. Correction is pleasanter. For then I have glimpses of what I was passing through as I wrote.

Thomas's growing preference for instinctual writing, and for an avoidance of explanation or obvious deliberation, is reflected in his approach to the task of anthologising, as recorded in his editorial correspondence with Grant Richards. On 8 November 1906, in reference to his work on *The Pocket Book of Poems and Songs for the Open Air*, Thomas writes: 'for my own part I do not see why such a book should be burdened with critical refuse & I have therefore said nothing at all but have left the tunes to take care of themselves which they are beautiful & strong enough to do'.

Thomas's preference for instinctual writing is strengthened by a 1913 experience of poetic composition. A letter of 7 September 1913 to Walter de la Mare supplies the detail of an aborted attempt at writing poetry, also investigated in Thomas's essay 'Insomnia'. In both accounts he places emphasis on the debilitating effect of deliberation or compulsion on the creative process, writing in 'Insomnia' that

I was under a very strong compulsion. I could do no more; not a line would add itself to the wretched three; nor did they cease to return again and again to my head.

In the spring of 1915, he can be seen examining his processes in order to ensure that habit has not taken over, writing to John Freeman: 'Tell me if you see signs of a *habit of versifying*? Do I sometimes miss emphasis altogether?' He also criticises the work of other writers he had previously admired, such as Bottomley. In a letter of late November 1915 to Freeman he calls Bottomley's use of an image of snow 'stagey', coming 'of thinking about snow indoors', and in 10 June 1916 he writes to Frost of Bottomley's play *King Lear's Wife*: 'It is made up. B. had thought out the motives.'

In contrast, as he later observes to both Frost and Freeman in May and June 1915, Thomas believed that a successful writer (successful in an aesthetic sense) would experience no division between conception and execution. Two days before his 7 September 1913 letter to de la Mare, Thomas writes to Eleanor Farjeon that 'I can't yet do an autobiography – which will enable me to put my material in a continuous and united form instead of my usual patchwork. Can you help?' However, on 5 December 1913, Thomas records in a letter to her his discovery of a way to approach a union of conception and execution. He does this in the writing of *The Childhood of Edward Thomas* by capitalising on his tendency to excessive self-consciousness, and deliberately cultivating a method of composition that eschews intentional interference with the processes of his own writing. He reports these experiments in excited detail in his letters. On 8 December 1913 he notes to Farjeon that 'I scarcely allow myself any reflection or explanation' and in the same month to Freeman that 'I (at 35) interfere as little as possible.' On 16 December 1913 he writes to Farjeon that 'I feel the shape of the sentences & alter continually with some unseen end in view', and on 29 May 1914 he mentions the work to de la Mare, calling it 'a very bald thing in which I have not attempted to do more than record facts. No atmosphere, no explanation.' Given the emphasis on avoiding deliberation in this approach to composition, it seems likely that this, together with his experiment in poetry in September 1913 and the continuous writing methods he was obliged to employ in the composition of *Feminine Influence*, showed him the way forward to his mature verse.

Thomas's composing processes in poetry

Thomas's employment of instinctive gambits in order to evade the restrictions that a more conventional considered approach can impose is also evident in his poetic compositions, as indicated in a comment to de la Mare in early 1915: 'I wrote [my poetry] (if anything) with a feeling that I did use the Morse code. This is a fact.' A letter of 23 March 1915 to W.H. Hudson suggests Thomas preferred to discover the meaning of a poem after he had written it, feeling 'what one has written, and not what one meant'. There are also references to the potential creative use of chaotic or fragmented material gleaned from dreams, particularly in his employment of the word 'copyright' in a letter to de la Mare (29 March 1911):

I had a strange dream last night. It began with me crouching with a great fear of something I could not see but which I knew to be dragonish behind me & just about to grip me by the nape of the neck. Then someone I knew but could not see – & I don't know who – bent down & whispered in a terrific voice: 'He is in the orchard.' Then he bent nearer & whispered still lower & more terrific: 'There *is* no orchard.' This was so alarming in its signifi-

Edward Thomas's Poets

cance that I awoke. This is my copyright.

Another way in which Thomas circumvented his habits of excessive
introspection was to write when he was distracted, often composing
while another activity was going on. He was aware of this, remarking
on his tendency to compose while travelling home by train in the dark,
a habit that is incidentally reflected in his poems' frequent subject-
matter of roads, journeys and the search for a home. He writes to
Bottomley on 11 February 1916 that 'at weekends especially on my
way home I sometimes find I can make verses'. A 1916 letter to J.W.
Haines contains the intriguing information that for Thomas, dark-
ness, not sunshine, is conducive to poetic composition:

> I have not written much lately. We have shifted to a new hut with
> less comfort & quiet. Also the lack of leave means less opportunity
> for work, as I have found long railway journeys good reasons for
> writing what has collected in my mind, especially in the dark. Now
> as I travel home in sunshine I don't feel the least bit inclined.

Thomas also took the trouble to note on a number of drafts of
poems the mode of transport and destination of the journey during
which they were written, indicating the importance to him of the indi-
vidual circumstances in which particular poems were composed.
This is borne out by an examination of, for example, the conditions
in which 'Words' was written, while he was cycling up a hill in the
company of Haines, an amateur botanist, shortly before Thomas
decided to enlist, and at a time when he was engaged in epistolary
debate with Bottomley on Frost's theory of poetry. The poem names
a flower identified for him (wrongly) by Haines, and revolves around
the speaker's role as a poet, waiting to be elected by words that
'choose' him.

The importance to Thomas of physical dislocation as a means of
fostering his processes of composition is suggested, too, in his poem
'The sun used to shine'. A celebration of Thomas's friendship with
Frost, and also, perhaps, an evocation of his earlier walks and talks
with de la Mare, and with other friends, as celebrated in his *Light and
Twilight* essay 'The Stile', this poem can be read as a disquisition on
the subject of poetic composition. It refers not only to travel in the
form of walking, but also to talking, and the easy rhythms of intimate
speech are reflected in the description of the characters' rhythm of
walking.

Temporal shifts played a crucial part in Thomas's composition processes. He talks of the need to 'digest' a draft and to think over responses he receives from his correspondents before returning to a poem. However, perhaps following on from a procedure forced on him in the case of some of his prose works, written to such tight deadlines that there was no time for redrafting, he treats the drafting process with delicacy. He shows a reluctance to 'tinker' with his poems, as expressed to John Freeman in early 1915 with reference to 'The Barn and the Down', and his poems do not, he notes to Bottomley on 30 June 1915, 'get much correction on paper'.

Another way of circumventing a deliberate approach to writing is use of the unpredictable. Thomas talks approvingly of being surprised by the onset of his poetic composition processes. His poem 'Go now' suggests surprise is a crucial element in the composing process, an element he also perceives as essential in his life, as he writes to Frost on 19 October 1916: 'I think perhaps a man ought to be capable of always being surprised on being confronted with what he really is – as I am nowadays when I confront a full size mirror in a good light instead of a cracked bit of one in a dark barrack room.' Thomas integrates such surprise into what at that time were unorthodox experiments in rhyme and metre. These gave his poems an air of rough, unchiselled 'unfinish', as he terms it in a letter of 1 June 1915 to Jesse Berridge and in letters to Farjeon and Edward Garnett that refer to rhyme in 'After Rain' and to metre in 'Lob'. His criticism from his peers also focuses on this feature. In a letter to de la Mare dated 24 March 1915 he responds to de la Mare's observation that he has 'gone wrong over metre'; a letter of 22 May 1915 to Farjeon reports Bottomley as saying he is 'too much bound [by] my prose methods of statement'; and on 5 May 1915 his letter to Freeman relays comments received from Harold Monro and Vivian Locke Ellis: 'Two people have just told me my rhythm isn't obvious enough – my things are "eminently the stuff poetry is made of" etc.'

Thomas's preference for what is unfinished or unexpected may also be linked to his tendency to end poems with a line that involves a sudden switch in subject, as in 'Cock-Crow' and 'The long small room'; his custom of writing poems from the last line backwards, as in 'A Dream' and 'The long small room'; the intriguing inference that the reading process could begin 'backwards', as when he tells Freeman in December 1913 that his autobiography 'is best begun at the end'; his declared ambition to Freeman in a letter of 8 March 1915 to keep under twelve lines; and his emphasis on what is absent, unsaid or on an exact focus on the particular detail of what is usually overlooked, as in 'But these things also'.

Edward Thomas's Poets

Thomas's correspondence provides many illustrations of his interest in the vernacular, dialect, oral storytelling, proverbs, local place names and sounds of nature and, in particular, his interest in the 'vernacular' of local birdsong. This keen awareness of the sound of language is suggested by his use of his distinctive, idiosyncratically spaced orthography to indicate pace and rhythm. When the following page of comments on a draft of Thomas's novel *The Happy-go-lucky Morgans*, taken from a February 1913 letter to de la Mare, is laid out in an approximation of the spaced punctuation of the original, the emphasis on the quality of incompleteness is thrown into relief. This is significant since incompleteness is later celebrated by Thomas as 'unfinish' in his poetry. Thomas's use of space and underlining to separate the word 'impediments' suggests, too, the use of space as an almost physical obstacle:

```
see it    .  I leave it  to you .   I
have    2   further  chapters      ,
perhaps  good in  themselves,     but
only   impediments      like    all the
other   chapters .  I wont send them yet.
         Of course   I      should like  to
know   just   what  you   think
         useless
         incomplete   ( excessively )
         obscure
         inconsistent
  Has it    in  places  a    private
character    in a  bad sense   ,
preventing   readers  from  sharing
my knowledge  ,  real  or  pretended ?
Does the tendency  to be  continuous
in the last   few chapters    (about
Philip )   only   show up    the
```

Thomas's focus on the sound of language, on the unfinished roughness of the spoken vernacular and on oral traditions is present in substantial parts of his prose books as well as in his poetry, and so creates a link between the two. This is especially the case in works such as *Four-and-Twenty Blackbirds* and 'Lob'. Both these works weave together the rhythms, meaning and contexts of vernacular sayings.

Thomas's letters record his fascination with the voice and oral experiments of children, in particular his youngest daughter's naïve and unrestrained experiments with language and metre that favour rhyme, rhythm and melody over sense. On 14 August 1914 he writes to John Freeman from Ledington, where he was engaging in daily conversations with Frost about speech and theories of poetry:

> She sang 4 to 5 verses of 'John Peel' the other morning with not one line of sense, yet using hardly one word that isn't in the song, just transposing & re-arranging, retaining only the tune & the metre. Some lines were better than sense, but I can't remember one.

This interest is reflected in Thomas's own use of irregular rhyme and unexpected metrical anomalies; his focus in his earlier poems on dialogue; and his emphasis on the ear rather than the eye, advising his readers to listen rather than look. It coincides with the start of his close friendship with Eleanor Farjeon, who was also very aware of the sounds and rhythms of the vernacular and children's rhymes. Her collection *Nursery Rhymes of London Town* (1916) draws heavily on nursery rhymes and local place names. In 1913 de la Mare's *Peacock Pie* was published, a book of rhymes that Thomas rated extremely highly, considering it second only to the work of Frost. He praised it for its effect on his daughters, when read aloud, writing to de la Mare's wife Elfie on 9 January 1917:

> When I was home on my last leave Bronwen & Baba were full of Peacock Pie. I wish Jack knew how much they liked to hear it read through. I don't know any poet who could give such perfect pleasure.

It is no accident that in response to de la Mare's adverse criticism of Thomas's poetry, Thomas focuses on its sound, musicality and 'accent': 'I only hope someone beside myself will catch the accent. They all seemed speakable tho none chantable.'

As well as contributing to an understanding of his poetic processes, Thomas's letters provide biographical detail to some of the poems, such as 'Snow' and 'Home [2]', and records of the conditions in which he wrote some of them. As noted earlier, the letters reveal that 'Words' was partly written while cycling up and down the hills of Gloucestershire, when Thomas was in the final throes of a decision about whether to enlist or go to America. A reflection of these conditions can be seen in the twisty, broken lines of the poem and its syntactical shifts between and across the lines, suggesting a close link between immediate physical and environmental conditions and the process of composition.

Thomas repeatedly comments, too, on connections between sensations of boredom, confinement and sickness and poetic composition. One of his most prolific periods as a poet occurs when he is confined to the house with an injured ankle. A letter to Frost on 12 October 1915 shows his awareness of his tendency to write when suffering physical confinement: 'I don't write now. Perhaps I should if I had an interval as I did when my foot was bad.' In a later letter to Frost, on 15 August 1916, he attempts to explain this phenomenon as a way of forcing the concentration necessary for composition to occur: 'I wrote some lines after a period in hospital – largely because to concentrate is the only happy thing possible when one is bored & helpless.'

⋆

Edward Thomas's Poets contains letters on his poetry written by Thomas to nine of his literary friends. On at least two occasions Thomas destroyed many of his papers when moving house. As a result, although his side of his correspondence has generally been carefully preserved, few of the letters to him have survived. In the case of letters to Haines and Hudson, often only extracts remain.

In this book, Thomas's own poems remain the chief 'subject'. Letters discussing or illuminating his poems are interleaved with the relevant poems and also with poems by his correspondents that pre-date or were written concurrently with his, and which are particularly pertinent to Thomas's pieces. These include some poems by W.H. Davies, who lived closely with Thomas for a number of years and whose poetry Thomas clearly admired, and poems by another associate, Lascelles Abercrombie. Echoes of poems by other contemporaries are also noted, either in the text or in the endnotes.

The Appendix 'Letters on the Poetic Process' contains more general letters from Thomas on his composing process and poetic output, ordered chronologically. This is followed by brief accounts of Thomas's main literary friends featured in this book.

The specific focus of *Edward Thomas's Poets* on Thomas's processes of poetic composition presents a model for books approaching poems as process and re-embedding them in their complex occasions and relations. It also offers a way of reading Thomas anew. By relating Thomas's letters on the process of poetic composition to specific poems and interleaving his poems with works by his contemporaries and friends, many of whom he reviewed, the book not only illuminates Thomas's development as a poet but contributes sculpturally to an understanding of him as a writer, approaching him from various perspectives, reflected in different relationships. New interpretations of his poems are revealed, adding substantially to an understanding of Thomas's *oeuvre*. Thomas is contextualised in his time, as a writer who breaks free from the constraints of his day, but also as a writer who is closely situated within it, issuing forth from it, carrying echoes of his contemporaries' work with him. Thomas's own possible response to such an evaluation can be divined in comments in a letter of 6 June 1902 to Jesse Berridge, written after receiving a response to his volume of essays *Horae Solitariae*: '"Echo" is a good word & a fine & I hope a true piece of criticism. I quite understand & wish I could be sure I deserved it.'

A Note on the Texts

The main sources of the Edward Thomas correspondence are:

Jesse Berridge *Edward Thomas's Letters to Jesse Berridge*, ed. Anthony Berridge (London: Enitharmon, 1983)

Gordon Bottomley *Letters from Edward Thomas to Gordon Bottomley*, ed. R.G. Thomas (London: Oxford University Press, 1968)
'Letters to Gordon Bottomley', *Edward Thomas Fellowship Newsletter*, 55 (January 2006), 10–18

Walter de la Mare Bodleian Library, Letters to Walter de la Mare, MS Eng lett c 376

Eleanor Farjeon Battersea Public Library Local History Department, Edward Thomas Manuscript Collection
Edward Thomas: The Last Four Years (Oxford: Oxford University Press, 1958)

John Freeman British Library, Letters to John Freeman, MS RP 1791
'To John Freeman', *Edward Thomas Fellowship Newsletter*, 32 (February 1995), 12–13
'The Letters of Edward Thomas to John Freeman', *Edward Thomas Fellowship Newsletter*, 38 (January 1998), 3–17

Robert Frost *Elected Friends: Robert Frost & Edward Thomas to One Another*, ed. Matthew Spencer (New York: Handsel Books, 2003)

Edward Garnett *A Selection of Letters to Edward Garnett*, originally in *Athenaeum* 16 and 23 (April 1920), ed. Edward Garnett (Edinburgh: Tragara Press, 1981)
'To Edward Garnett', *Edward Thomas Fellow-*

	ship Newsletter, 52 (August 2004), 12–17, 30 (January 1994), 10–11
J.W. Haines	Bodleian Library, Copies of E Thomas's Letters, MS Eng letters c 280, items 154–8 Bodleian Library, R. Ingpen and J.W. Haines Letters, MS Eng lett c 281
W.H. Hudson	'Edward Thomas's letters to W.H. Hudson', *The London Mercury*, 1920, II.10 (August 1920), 434–42 'To W.H. Hudson', *Edward Thomas Fellowship Newsletter*, 52 (August 2004), 6–12

Additional letters are in *Edward Thomas: Selected Letters*, ed. R.G. Thomas (Oxford: Oxford University Press, 1995); *Letters to Helen*, ed. R.G. Thomas (Manchester: Carcanet Press, 2000); and *The Life and Letters of Edward Thomas*, ed. John Moore (London: Heinemann, 1939). Quotations from Thomas's poetry are from R.G. Thomas's 1978 edition of *The Collected Poems of Edward Thomas*, the titles mostly those of R.G. Thomas's edition, but some alternative commonly used titles have been added, mostly from Edna Longley's *Poems and Last Poems*. Where numbers in square brackets follow a title, as in 'An Old Song [1]', this follows R.G. Thomas's convention and indicates which of several poems by Thomas with the same title is being cited. Other detail includes date and place of composition, and Thomas's manuscript notes on the circumstances of composition, usually comprising location and direction or destination of travel. Some of Thomas's friends had similar names. In this book, Farjeon, Freeman and Haines refer to Eleanor Farjeon, John Freeman and J.W. Haines. A. Martin Freeman's name is written in full. References in his letters to 'Helen' are to Thomas's wife. Thomas also refers to his son Mervyn (sometimes written with the Welsh spelling Merfyn), born 1900, and his daughters Bronwen, born 1902, and Myfanwy (Baba), born 1910. 'Steep' is the village in Hampstead, in or near which Thomas and his family lived in various houses from 1906 to 1916. Occasionally previously published letters of Thomas include misreadings of his handwriting. Where this is obviously the case, these have been corrected. Where extracts are included, the omissions are indicated by three asterisks. The underlining in Thomas's handwritten letters has been printed here as italic.

Edward Thomas's Poets

Acknowledgements

For advice and encouragement, thanks go to the Edward Thomas Fellowship, particularly Richard Emeny and Anne Harvey, also to Dr Anne Bentinck Roger and Jeff Cooper, Professor Peter Childs, Professor Edna Longley, Professor Peter Widdowson of Cyder Press, and Pamela Blevins. The resources of the Oxford Bodleian Library, the Cambridge University Library, the British Library and the Battersea Public Library Local History Department in London and the University of Gloucestershire Archives; the untiring advice and support of the librarians at these institutions; and the practical support of Professor David and Diana Kendall, Eleanor Kercher, Andy Kilmister, Alex Lipinski and Linda Yeaton on visits to these institutions, were essential to the completion of this work. Helpful and stimulating discussion on initial ideas on processes of composing with Dr Alan Brown, Professor Simon Dentith, Professor Philip Gross, Dr Martin Randall and Dr Shelley Saguaro; the enthusiasm with which Michael Schmidt embraced this project; and the kind and patient support of Judith Willson are in a large part responsible for the conception and execution of *Edward Thomas's Poets*.

Grateful thanks go to the estate of Myfanwy Thomas for permission to make use of material relating to Edward Thomas. Acknowledgements are also due to Duckworth Publishers for permission to reprint an extract from Michael Fairless's *The Roadmender*; Jeff Cooper for advice on texts by Lascelles Abercrombie and permission to reprint these; the Society of Authors and the estate of Walter de la Mare for permission to reprint poems by Walter de la Mare; David Higham Associates and the estate of Eleanor Farjeon for permission to reprint writings of Eleanor Farjeon; and Henry Holt & Co. and the estate of Robert Frost for permission to reprint writings of Robert Frost. Every effort has been made to trace the copyright of other texts appearing in this book, but without success. Apologies are therefore due for the omission of acknowledgements in these cases. The editor and publishers would be glad to correct any omissions in future editions.

Edward Thomas's Poets

I can write back as easily as a wall makes an echo
Edward Thomas to Gordon Bottomley, Rose Acre,
17 October 1902

1914

November Sky (November)

November's days are thirty:
November's earth is dirty,
Those thirty days, from first to last;
And the prettiest things on ground are the paths
With morning and evening hobnails dinted,
With foot and wing-tip overprinted
Or separately charactered,
Of little beast and little bird.
The fields are mashed by sheep, the roads
Make the worst going, the best the woods
Where dead leaves upward and downward scatter.
Few care for the mixture of earth and water,
Twig, leaf, flint, thorn,
Straw, feather, all that men scorn,
Pounded up and sodden by flood,
Condemned as mud.

But of all the months when earth is greener
Not one has clean skies that are cleaner.
Clean and clear and sweet and cold,
They shine above the earth so old,
While the after-tempest cloud
Sails over in silence though winds are loud,
Till the full moon in the east
Looks at the planet in the west
And earth is silent as it is black,
Yet not unhappy for its lack.
Up from the dirty earth men stare:
One imagines a refuge there

Above the mud, in the pure bright
Of the cloudless heavenly light:
Another loves earth and November more dearly
Because without them, he sees clearly,
The sky would be nothing more to his eye
Than he, in any case, is to the sky;
He loves even the mud whose dyes
Renounce all brightness to the skies.

Letter to Robert Frost, 15 December 1914

Thomas had already sent Frost 'November Sky' for comment.
A typescript of this poem held with Frost's papers in Dartmouth
College Library has the following variations – 'And in amongst
them clearly printed /The foot's seal and the wing's light word'
(lines 6-7), and 'Only odd men (who do not matter)/ Care for'
(lines 10–11).

Dear Frost,   Steep, 15 December 1914

I am glad you spotted 'wing's light word'. I knew it was wrong & also
that many would like it; also 'odd men' – a touch nearing facetious-
ness in it. I've got rid of both now. But I am in it & no mistake. I have
an idea I am full enough but that my bad habits and customs and
duties of writing will make it rather easy to write when I've no busi-
ness to. At the same time I find myself engrossed & conscious of a
possible perfection as I never was in prose. Also I'm very impatient
of my prose, & of reviews & of review books. And yet I have been
uncommonly cheerful mostly. I have been rather pleased with some
of the pieces of course, but it's not wholly that. Still, I won't begin
thanking you just yet, tho if you like I will put it down now that you
are the only begetter right enough.

I should like to see the man who was upset by you rhyming 'come'
& 'dumb'. I should also like to write about you for the 'Forum'. But
they wouldn't want me to, I feel quite sure. Only I will write to them
just to see.

You speak of your 'few remaining weeks here.' But that doesn't
mean any early move, does it whether you only leave Ryton or go
back home. Scott sails tomorrow. He was willing to take Mervyn over
& tutor him. He was to be learning blacksmithery & would teach
Mervyn (if Mervyn would learn). But Mervyn hasn't gone, didn't
much want to, while the proposal was a little too sudden tho I had the

feeling it might be god's idea to get Mervyn away from me for ever that way.

Mervyn is to have Peter for company this Christmas probably. We are expecting him instead of the Dutch boy

My works come pouring in on you just now. Tell me all you dare about them. I have been shy of blank verse tho (or because) I like it best. But the rhymes have dictated themselves decidedly except in one case.

I gather that Marsh is more or less engrossed now & reckoned not to be approachable, but I don't know whether to believe it. In town I saw de la Mare & that is what he said. But he & I have withdrawn from one another I fancy. At least I know I am never myself so long as I am with him. Now I have put it to Monro that he might show 'North of Boston' to E.M. We'll see.

I wish you were a day's walk away or were really at anchor.

Yours ever
E.T.

March

Steep, 5 December 1914

Now I know that Spring will come again,
Perhaps tomorrow: however late I've patience
After this night following on such a day.

While still my temples ached from the cold burning
Of hail and wind, and still the primroses
Torn by the hail were covered up in it,
The sun filled earth and heaven with a great light
And a tenderness, almost warmth, where the hail dripped,
As if the mighty sun wept tears of joy.
But 'twas too late for warmth. The sunset piled
Mountains on mountains of snow and ice in the west:
Somewhere among their folds the wind was lost,
And yet 'twas cold, and though I knew that Spring
Would come again, I knew it had not come,
That it was lost, too, in those mountains cold.

What did the thrushes know? Rain, snow, sleet, hail,
Had kept them quiet as the primroses.
They had but an hour to sing. On boughs they sang,
On gates, on ground; they sang while they changed perches
And while they fought, if they remembered to fight:
So earnest were they to pack into that hour
Their unwilling hoard of song before the moon
Grew brighter than the clouds. Then 'twas no time
For singing merely. So they could keep off silence
And night, they cared not what they sang or screamed,
Whether 'twas hoarse or sweet or fierce or soft,
And to me all was sweet: they could do no wrong.
Something they knew – I also, while they sang
And after. Not till night had half its stars
And never a cloud, was I aware of silence
Rich with all that riot of songs, a silence
Saying that Spring returns, perhaps tomorrow.

Edward Thomas's Poets

W.H. Davies, 'In May', *Songs of Joy and Others* **(London: A.C. Fifield, 1911)**

In a *Daily Chronicle* review of 30 January 1912, Thomas praised W.H. Davies's *Songs of Joy* for commanding 'the pellucid, fresh, and sweet in which he has no equal or competitor'. Davies's 'In May', like Thomas's 'March', describes the urgency of bird-song, the birds packing their song into a short space of time.

> Yes, I will spend the livelong day
> With Nature in this month of May;
> And sit beneath the trees, and share
> My bread with birds whose homes are there;
> While cows lie down to eat, and sheep
> Stand to their necks in grass so deep;
> While birds do sing with all their might,
> As though they felt the earth in flight.
> This is the hour I dreamed of, when
> I sat surrounded by poor men;
> And thought of how the Arab sat
> Alone at evening, gazing at
> The stars that bubbled in clear skies;
>
> And of young dreamers, when their eyes
> Enjoyed methought a precious boon
> In the adventures of the Moon
> Whose light, behind the Clouds' dark bars,
> Searched for her stolen flocks of stars.
> When I, hemmed in by wrecks of men,
> Thought of some lonely cottage then,
> Full of sweet books; and miles of sea,
> With passing ships, in front of me;
> And having, on the other hand,
> A flowery, green, bird-singing land.

After Rain

Steep, 14 December 1914

The rain of a night and a day and a night
Stops at the light
Of this pale choked day. The peering sun
Sees what has been done.
The road under the trees has a border new
Of purple hue
Inside the border of bright thin grass:
For all that has
Been left by November of leaves is torn
From hazel and thorn
And the greater trees. Throughout the copse
No dead leaf drops
On grey grass, green moss, burnt-orange fern,
At the wind's return:
The leaflets out of the ash-tree shed
Are thinly spread
In the road, like little black fish, inlaid,
As if they played.
What hangs from the myriad branches down there
So hard and bare
Is twelve yellow apples lovely to see
On one crab-tree,
And on each twig of every tree in the dell
Uncountable
Crystals both dark and bright of the rain
That begins again.

Letters to Eleanor Farjeon, 10 and 16 January 1915

Eleanor Farjeon typed many of Thomas's manuscript poems
for him. The resultant exchange of letters often included discussions of individual lines. In these letters Thomas refers to 'After
Rain', and also 'The Interval' and 'An Old Song [1]' ('I was not
apprenticed nor ever dwelt in famous Lincolnshire').

My dear Eleanor,   Steep, 10 January 1915

Thank you for your letter. This is simply just to say there is no hurry for returning the MS. It was interesting to find you prefer my remarks unrhymed. You hit upon some passages I felt doubtful. 'But 'under storm's wing' was not just for the metre. 'As if they played' I was anxious to have in. It describes the patterns of the fish but it comes awkwardly perhaps after inlaid. I mean in 'Interval' that the night did postpone her coming a bit for the twilight. Night might have been expected to come down on the end of day but didn't. 'Held off' would have been stricter. As to 'sing and whistle first', I don't think 'to whistle and to sing' which is formally correct is as good. If I am consciously doing anything I am trying to get rid of the last rags of rhetoric and formality which left my prose so often with a dead rhythm only. If I can be honest and am still bad in rhythm it will be because I am bad in rhythm.

Now I am downstairs but worse off because I know how helpless I still am [with a sprained ankle]. I can only hop and am in a filthy temper and couldn't enjoy Stanley's song at all. I never heard it before.

I hope your mother is better this fine frosty morning.

Yours ever

E.T.

My dear Eleanor   Steep, 16 January 1915

Thank you very much for these copies. I now have some later pieces you shall see when you come back, and I do appreciate having a safe in Hampstead in a road which the flashlight opposite thinks as safe as Berlin, I suppose. So you really are going to Ryton. How I wish I could. I am glad your mother is well enough and hope she took the soup. As to the party for Maitland it is most likely I shouldn't be free by then to any extent. I get on too slowly and am not sure I do get on. I had a setback owing to a slip. And if I am better by then I must try to get to the Frosts. I should like to see you and Viola Meynell and Maitland but a crowd is a crowd for me, I am afraid.

I am pleased you like 'After Rain' best. I wonder whether I can do anything with 'inlaid' and 'played'. The inlaid, too, is at any rate perfectly precise as I saw the black leaves 2 years ago up at the top of the hill, so that neither is a rhyme word only. No, I don't believe rhyme is at all a *bad* trouble. I use it now more often than not and always fancy I leave the rhymed pieces as easy as the rest, but tho I am so young a versifier I don't pretend to be sure.

The children are just beginning school again. We have had a lot of cards together after supper but not one walk. Baba has been very good. The other morning I told her I had dreamed about Frost. Do you mean the man Frost? she said. I used to draw for her when I was horizontal; now I do nothing for nobody.

Yours ever
Edward Thomas

The Interval

Steep, mid-December 1914 [?]

Gone the wild day.
A wilder night
Coming makes way
For brief twilight.

Where the firm soaked road
Mounts beneath pines
To the high beech wood
It almost shines.

The beeches keep
A stormy rest,
Breathing deep
Of wind from the west.

The wood is black,
With a misty steam.
Above it the rack
Breaks for one gleam.

But the woodman's cot
By the ivied trees
Awakens not
To light or breeze.

It smokes aloft
Unwavering:
It hunches soft
Under storm's wing.

It has no care
For gleam or gloom:
It stays there
While I shall roam,

Die and forget
The hill of trees,
The gleam, the wet,
This roaring peace.

1914

Walter de la Mare, 'Mrs. MacQueen', *Peacock Pie* (London: Constable, 1913)

Thomas rated *Peacock Pie* extremely highly, and had long admired 'Mrs. MacQueen'. The gleam of Mrs MacQueen's candle, the emphasis on the linden tree, the 'roar of the distant sea', the gathering darkness and the brief four-line stanzas all recall Thomas's own 'Interval'.

> With glass like a bull's-eye,
>   And shutters of green,
> Down on the cobbles
>   Lives Mrs. MacQueen.
>
> At six she rises;
>   At nine you see
> Her candle shine out
>   In the linden tree:
>
> And at half-past nine
>   Not a sound is nigh,
> But the bright moon's creeping
>   Across the sky;
>
> Or a far dog baying;
>   Or a twittering bird
> In its drowsy nest,
>   In the darkness stirred;
>
> Or like the roar
>   Of a distant sea,
> A long-drawn *S-s-sh!*
>   In the linden tree.

Letter to Walter de la Mare, 4 November 1908 (extracts)

Most of the verses Thomas praises here, including 'Mrs. MacQueen', later appeared in either *The Listeners* or *Peacock Pie*.

My dear de la Mare,   4 November 1908

I am sorry to have to put off coming especially as it is on account of your wife – I do hope she will soon be really well again & that your fears are disappointed. I have hurried through the poems at once & liked many of them but chiefly

Never-to-be
An Epitaph
'Be gentle, O hands of a child'
'No sound over the deep'
'Nod'
'Mrs. McQueen'

& rather less: –

The stranger
'Or to take arms'
After 'The Dynasts'

By the way I never feel sure about your way of dividing up such lines, but I feel sure that in the last verse of 'The Dynasts' it is faulty & you really could write the verse in eight lines or in a dozen other ways. But it is lines that end on an unaccented syllable that look badly wrong

***

I think these pieces are up to all but your very best & you ought to send them out with confidence.

My wife would like to come over & see your wife & *the children*, but she comes so seldom to town that the time may be full up on her possible visit before Christmas. I will let you know later on.

How is the monkey's tale?

Yours ever

Edward Thomas

The Mountain Chapel

Steep, mid-December 1914 [?]

Chapel and gravestones, old and few,
Are shrouded by a mountain fold
From sound and view
Of life. The loss of the brook's voice
Falls like a shadow. All they hear is
The eternal noise
Of wind whistling in grass more shrill
Than aught as human as a sword,
And saying still:
"'Tis but a moment since man's birth,
And in another moment more
Man lies in earth
For ever; but I am the same
Now, and shall be, even as I was
Before he came:
Till there is nothing I shall be.'

Yet there the sun shines after noon
So cheerfully
The place almost seems peopled, nor
Lacks cottage chimney, cottage hearth:
It is not more
In size than is a cottage, less
Than any other empty home
In homeliness.
It has a garden of wild flowers
And finest grass and gravestones warm
In sunshine hours
The year through. Men behind the glass
Stand once a week, singing, and drown
The whistling grass
Their ponies munch. And yet somewhere
Near or far off there's some man could
Live happy here,
Or one of the gods perhaps, were they
Not of inhuman stature dire
As poets say
Who have not seen them clearly, if

At sound of any wind of the world
In grass-blades stiff
They would not startle and shudder cold
Under the sun. When Gods were young
This wind was old.

Verses four and five from W.H. Hudson, 'In the Wilderness',
Merry England, **1883–5, in** *Dead Man's Plack, An Old Thorn*
and Poems **(London: Dent, 1924)**

Hudson's description of grass-blades as spears in this long poem
is reflected in Thomas's swords of grass in 'The Mountain
Chapel', in 'Tall reeds / Like criss-cross bayonets' in his 'The
Pond' (also known as 'Bright Clouds') and in 'long bayonet-like
reeds' in his essay 'Birds of March' (written in 1895).

There winds would sing to me, the old,
Old sea give forth a solemn sound,
    The wild birds warble mirth;
There would I stop to kiss the ground
    For very love of earth
And swift away the years would glide,
    Like rills that have their birth
High on the soaring mountain side.

To gaze upon the prospect wide,
Oft on some jutting crag I'd lie
    When blooms its summer crown –
Pale heath and pansy's purple eye,
    The wind-flower, and the brown
And green blades of the bearded grass,
    Whose spears wave up and down,
White sparkling when the wind doth pass.

The Manor Farm

Steep, 24 December 1914

The rock-like mud unfroze a little and rills
Ran and sparkled down each side of the road
Under the catkins wagging in the hedge.
But earth would have her sleep out, spite of the sun;
Nor did I value that thin gilding beam
More than a pretty February thing
Till I came down to the old Manor Farm,
And church and yew-tree opposite, in age
Its equals and in size. Small church, great yew,
And farmhouse slept in a Sunday silentness.
The air raised not a straw. The steep farm roof,
With tiles duskily glowing, entertained
The midday sun; and up and down the roof
White pigeons nestled. There was no sound but one.
Three cart-horses were looking over a gate
Drowsily through their forelocks, swishing their tails
Against a fly, a solitary fly.

The Winter's cheek flushed as if he had drained
Spring, Summer, and Autumn at a draught
And smiled quietly. But 'twas not Winter –
Rather a season of bliss unchangeable
Awakened from farm and church where it had lain
Safe under tile and thatch for ages since
This England, Old already, was called Merry.

Letters to Edward Garnett and W.H. Hudson, 13 and 23 March 1915

These letters reflect the high esteem in which Thomas held Garnett as a critic and Hudson as a writer. The letter to Garnett also identifies the place described in 'The Manor Farm' as the village Prior's Dean. Thomas had previously taken Garnett's criticism of his prose very much to heart, but in this letter he displays a new confidence in his poetry.

Edward Thomas's Poets

My dear Garnett   Steep, 13 March 1915

Thank you for your letter and your criticism, which I can mostly
agree with, except I think the line

England, old already, was called Merry

looks more eccentric than it is & sounds. I like that piece best perhaps.
But I don't think I could alter 'Tears' to make it marketable. I feel that
the correction you want made is only essential if the whole point is in
the British Grenadiers, as might be expected in these times. I can't be
sure about the jog trot. Perhaps you are right in finding it at the end
of 'November' where it gets a shade sententious & perhaps echoes
the end of [Shelley's] 'The Sensitive Plant' in rhythm.

I am now sending you the greater part of what I have done since I
began, including the very first, which is the longest one placed at the
end, called 'Up in the Wind'. I hope you will forgive me and survive
the swamping. You cannot imagine how eagerly I have run up this
byway and how anxious I am to be sure it is not a cul de sac.

I did the article you suggested and am sending it to the *Nation* first.
Yours ever
Edward Thomas

My dear Hudson,   Steep, Petersfield, 23 March 1915

I believe that a man who likes poetry and says honestly what he likes
is about as rare as a good critic, and I am really not sure if the two are
one. At any rate, apart from one or two such men, I don't know where
to look for the critic, so that as far as getting into his hands and having
his opinion go, I am not in a hurry to be published.

So far as I know reviewers, there are kind and complimentary ones,
there are enemies, and there are idiots besides. They have the power
to tickle or sting for a moment, but nothing more. They (*we*, I should
say) have to show how much cleverer they are than the reviewed. It
is so much easier to do this with offence. I would rather never do it
again, and I am certainly not anxious to be the victim of it as a versi-
fier. I had quite enough ups and downs reading your letter first,
though I was really very glad of it all. I was glad you liked 'After Rain'
and 'The Signpost'. (I will type 'The Signpost' and 'Beauty' for you
gladly) and glad to have your reasons for not wholly liking some
others. I must think about the sensation at the end of 'May 20'. I think
perhaps it must come out. But about 'Merry' in 'The Manor Farm',

I rather think I will stick to it. If one can feel what one has written, and not what one *meant*. I feel here as if the *merry* England asleep at Prior's Dean added to the sleepiness and enriched it somehow.

I am sending them about and getting them back. Probably I shall soon tire and be glad to consign them to a printed book.

If I had been coming up today I would have telegraphed. But I thought I would wait till next week. It is very good gardening weather and has been for a week now, and in fact good for everything except walking far. It has got very languid after a little rain following on nights of frost and days of sun. I shall be at the Mt Blanc, so far as I can tell, next Tuesday, or at 3 Henrietta St at 1: if you are to be, I will be. And I hope you will be better.

Looking back it seems possible you might think I had found your letter too critical. But really I would very much rather know that you like or don't wholly like a thing than that somebody else thinks it a pity I ever read Frost, etc.

Yours ever

E. Thomas

Edward Thomas's Poets

1915

The Source

Steep, 4 January 1915

All day the air triumphs with its two voices
Of wind and rain:
As loud as if in anger it rejoices,
Drowning the sound of earth
That gulps and gulps in choked endeavour vain
To swallow the rain.

Half the night, too, only the wild air speaks
With wind and rain,
Till forth the dumb source of the river breaks
And drowns the rain and wind,
Bellows like a giant bathing in mighty mirth
The triumph of earth.

Gordon Bottomley, 'Song II' from 'Night and Morning Songs' (1896–1909), *Chambers of Imagery* **II (London: Elkin Mathews, 1912)**

> Like 'The Source', this poem also bears a resemblance to Thomas's 'The New House' and 'Wind and Mist'.

I am tired of the wind –
Oh, wind, wind, be quiet ...
I am burdened by the days
Of wailing and long riot.
The heavy trees are thinned;
The clouds lose their ways ...
There's no rest in my mind.

When the wind falls the rain falls;
The air has no more breath.
The ceaseless 'Hush' of rain
Is what eternity saith.
The hills grown near and tall
Let down a misty mane ...
Endlessness weighs on all.

Letter to Gordon Bottomley, Christmas 1912

Thomas was very sensitive to wind and rain, as is made clear in
a number of letters to Gordon Bottomley. Here, amid quota-
tions from Shakespeare, Thomas suggests mythological
readings of heavy rain that are similar to those present in 'The
Source'.

My dear Gordon,   Wick Green, Friday, Christmas-time 1912

Thank you. I shall gladly carry the 100 Best Latin poems from
Gordon Bottomley about with me until they or I get worn out. I hope
my parcel didn't bring pure gloom to you. If not I will send another
soon. And I will come myself before very long. I can't quite say when.
I hope you are out of bed. Yet what could you do if you were? The
rain up here is incredible. It is like living before the creation, like the
Niflheim that men ultimately emerged from: – when will they come?
– We expect Davies today some time from Wales unless Swansea's
defeat of the South Africans has been too much for him. – I wish I
could have your hunting *Pleur du cerf* out of the woods below us.
Goodbye – a great while ago the world began & still the rain it raineth
every day. With our love to Emily & yourself
    Ever yours
    Edward Thomas

Edward Thomas's Poets

Snow

Steep, 7 January 1915

In the gloom of whiteness,
In the great silence of snow,
A child was sighing
And bitterly saying: 'Oh,
They have killed a white bird up there on her nest,
The down is fluttering from her breast.'
And still it fell through that dusky brightness
On the child crying for the bird of the snow.

Walter de la Mare, 'Snow', *Peacock Pie* (London: Constable, 1913)

No breath of wind,
No gleam of sun –
Still the white snow
Whirls softly down –
Twig and bough
And blade and thorn
All in an icy
Quiet, forlorn.
Whispering, rustling,
Through the air,
On sill and stone,
Roof – everywhere,
It heaps its powdery
Crystal flakes,
Of every tree
A mountain makes;
Till pale and faint
At shut of day,
Stoops from the West
One wintry ray.
And, feathered in fire,
Where ghosts the moon,
A robin shrills
His lonely tune.

Letter to Walter de la Mare, 24 November 1913

In this letter, written in praise of de la Mare's *Peacock Pie*,
Thomas describes his own *Four-and-Twenty Blackbirds*, a book
of retold proverbs, as feathers of falling snow. *Four-and-Twenty
Blackbirds* came out of stories Thomas told his children, and his
poem 'Snow' is written from a child's perception.

My dear de la Mare,   Steep, Petersfield, 24 November 1913

No it didn't tire me & if it did it would be without resentment. I
suppose country habits & the custom of going early to bed after fairly
hard days of walking or riding makes me rather under after 10, or it
may be simple mental infecundity. I shall come again as soon as I can,
perhaps Monday Oct. 6th, which at any rate is the earliest possible
day. Till then I am here writing about Ecstasy, good Lord, but
spending the Saturday & Sunday nights (4th & 5th) at Monro's.

Thank you for what you have done with W.H., & I will wait the 2
weeks. Even if he decides to keep the MSS I assume he will not object
to my serialising – it is just possible I could do so, & I have some small
confidence in the little things. They are not featherweight though. I
believe you take the featherweight as my label. I thought rather of
snow feathers coming down from above not bantam or goose feathers
blown up & down again. So I should have said gossamer, which has
an earthly conception but a heavenly generation. I wish I could say
how much I like it; but simple things are beyond my saying. Well I
am glad you have liked the series as I have liked the gossamers & their
autumns, & something more than that too, at Anerly & Harting &
Cowden.

Good luck
Yours ever
E.T.

Letter to Eleanor Farjeon, 6 January 1915

A biographical basis for the choice of a child's perception in
'Snow' can be found in Thomas's comments in this letter,
written the day before 'Snow'. Laid up with an injured ankle, he
is looking after his youngest child, 'Baba' or Myfanwy, and
refers to her experimental efforts at poetry.

        Edward Thomas's Poets

My dear Eleanor,   Steep, 6 January 1915

Letters seem the luxuries they are now. I am in bed or in the same position in a deck chair for a week or so and then probably a fortnight indoors but downstairs. So the Doctor says, but the sprain is looking better and feeling quite easy now. When the articles come to be written I shall have got used to the position I expect.

I am so sorry Rosalind is ill and you robbed of your holiday for the time being. You couldn't go to Ryton earlier could you? Frost hasn't been well and is rather low. But the others must be in good form with your Christmas box and all. They are good at Christmas. We had all surprises and I had a beautiful letter from Lesley about the Leadon in flood and the shiny nights. Now Baba has to be consoled by drawing. She has been crying without pretending.

Now I have drawn the 3 blind mice running after the farmers Wife.

I did afflict you with Young in spite of sending you a cut copy. I believe you read him straight through and endured all his 'cumulance of repose' and his meaningless metricalities. But L'Isolée has something good in it and 'The Cragsman' (is it so called?). Probably he is faddy about capitals on classic precedents. Much of the good editions of Roman poets begin a line with capitals only after full stops.

If you don't go to Wisbech or Ryton this week could you come here for a little while. It could and would be contrived gladly. If you don't come do you feel able to put into words anything you thought (before being asked by me) about England, say in connection with any part of it or any event or saying or person? Please don't *trouble* about it as troubling would probably produce what I don't want – I had some delicious humbug from a friend who discovered he couldn't *love* his country because he depended on her for his living. I didn't want his intelligent discoveries.

Baba rhymes verse regardless of sense and makes verse without rhyme and equally without sense for a long time on end nowadays.

Yours ever
E.T.

The Lofty Sky

Steep, 10 January 1915

Today I want the sky,
The tops of the high hills,
Above the last man's house,
His hedges, and his cows,
Where, if I will, I look
Down even on sheep and rook,
And of all the things that move
See buzzards only above: –
Past all trees, past furze
And thorn, where naught deters
The desire of the eye
For sky, nothing but sky.
I sicken of the woods
And all the multitudes
Of hedge-trees. They are no more
Than weeds upon this floor
Of the river of air
Leagues deep, leagues wide, where
I am like a fish that lives
In weeds and mud and gives
What's above him no thought.
I might be a tench for aught
That I can do today
Down on the wealden clay.
Even the tench has days
When he floats up and plays
Among the lily leaves
And sees the sky, or grieves
Not if he nothing sees:
While I, I know that trees
Under that lofty sky
Are weeds, fields mud, and I
Would arise and go far
To where the lilies are.

Edward Thomas's Poets

Walter de la Mare, 'Nobody Knows', *Peacock Pie* (London: Constable, 1913)

Both 'Nobody Knows' and Thomas's 'The Lofty Sky' describe the sky as a sea overhead. 'Nobody Knows' is written from the point of view of someone lying in bed, and 'The Lofty Sky' was composed while Thomas was prone with an injured ankle.

Often I've heard the Wind sigh
    By the ivied orchard wall,
Over the leaves in the dark night,
    Breathe a sighing call,
And faint away in the silence,
    While I, in my bed,
Wondered, 'twixt dreaming and waking,
        What it said.

Nobody knows what the Wind is,
    Under the height of the sky,
Where the hosts of the stars keep far away house
    And its wave sweeps by –
Just a great wave of the air,
    Tossing the leaves in its sea,
And foaming under the eaves of the roof
        That covers me.

And so we live under deep water,
    All of us, beasts and men,
And our bodies are buried down under the sand,
    When we go again;
And leave, like the fishes, our shells,
    And float on the Wind and away,
To where, o'er the marvellous tides of the air,
        Burns day.

Letter to Jesse Berridge, 6 January 1915

This letter reveals the conditions in which 'The Lofty Sky' and a number of other poems were composed – while Thomas was confined indoors with an injured ankle. The emphasis in 'The Lofty Sky' on life outdoors and a desire to escape appears to reflect these conditions.

My dear Jesse,   Steep, 6 January 1915

Will you please thank Dell for his letter to me & excuse me from
writing to you both because I am laid up for a time with a sprained
ankle & writing is not easy. But it is getting on well enough, thank
you.

I expect I have to congratulate you on your move to Brentwood,
as it must mean you have got the job you were telling me about. I am
very glad indeed, & shall be gladder if it means you can come here
for longer visits & makes Avebury as certain as possible. It looks as if
I shall remain in England all the year unless the war ends soon. If only
you could come down to give me Christian consolation in my
(moderate) distress! also to talk about England. I am writing an article
on what England means to people. I wonder could you give me any
thoughts you have had, the more intimate & purely your own the
better, – any thoughts symbolising England by any particular places,
persons, events, or words. I don't ask for an essay because I don't
want so much to know what you can think if you set yourself to as
what you habitually or instinctively or at some special moment have
felt. A short note would help, as I am prevented now while the essay
is being prepared from seeing & sending to anybody as I had
intended. I have no other work, but haven't begun to worry yet, as I
find I can go on doing work I want to do though nobody else wants
me to. I have even begun to write verse, but don't tell a soul, as if it
is to be published at all it must be anonymously.

A happy 1915 to you & Edna & all.

Yours ever

E.T.

Edward Thomas's Poets

The Owl

Steep, 24 February 1915

Downhill I came, hungry, and yet not starved;
Cold, yet had heat within me that was proof
Against the North wind; tired, yet so that rest
Had seemed the sweetest thing under a roof.

Then at the inn I had food, fire, and rest,
Knowing how hungry, cold, and tired was I.
All of the night was quite barred out except
An owl's cry, a most melancholy cry

Shaken out long and clear upon the hill,
No merry note, nor cause of merriment,
But one telling me plain what I escaped
And others could not, that night, as in I went.

And salted was my food, and my repose,
Salted and sobered, too, by the bird's voice
Speaking for all who lay under the stars,
Soldiers and poor, unable to rejoice.

from W.H. Hudson, *The Land's End* (London: Hutchinson, 1908)

The following extract from chapter 15 of Hudson's *The Land's End* forms a prose source of 'The Owl'. This book was reviewed by Thomas on 3 June 1908 in the *Daily Chronicle*, and in August 1908 in the *Bookman*, and discussed in *A Literary Pilgrim in England*, written in 1913–14 and published in 1917.

I went down the hill, chilled to the marrow, thinking of the birds asleep and occasionally disturbing one as I stumbled over the stones in the dark and picked my way among the black furze bushes. Indoors it was very comfortable, sitting by the fire, with the lighted lamp on the table and a book waiting to be read; then supper and a pipe, but through it all that strange and desolate aspect of nature remained persistently before my inner sight. I went to bed and lay soft and warm, covered with many blankets, but did not sleep; the wind increased in violence as the hours went on, making its doleful wailing and shrieking noises all round the house and causing the doors and windows to rattle in their frames. In spirit I was in it, out on the hill-side where the birds were in their secret hiding-places, in the black furze and heath, in holes and crevices in the hedges, their little hearts beating more languidly each hour, their eyes glazing, until stiff and dead they dropped from their perches.

W.H. Davies, 'The Owl', *Songs of Joy and Others* (London: A.C. Fifield, 1911)

In his *Daily Chronicle* review of Davies's *Songs of Joy* (30 January 1912), Thomas writes that 'The Owl' reaches 'a simplicity in which even the virtue of naïveté is left behind', and in his February 1912 *Bookman* review, he identifies it as one of Davies's 'simple, instanta-neous and new [poems], recalling older poets chiefly by their perfection'.

> The boding Owl, that in despair
>   Doth moan and shiver on warm nights –
> Shall that bird prophesy for me
>   The fall of Heaven's eternal lights?
>
> When in the thistled field of Age
>   I take my final walk on earth,
> Still will I make that Owl's despair
>   A thing to fill my heart with mirth.

The Child on the Cliff

Steep, 11 March 1915

Mother, the root of this little yellow flower
Among the stones has the taste of quinine.
Things are strange today on the cliff. The sun shines so bright,
And the grasshopper works at his sewing-machine
So hard. Here's one on my hand, mother, look;
I lie so still. There's one on your book.

But I have something to tell more strange. So leave
Your book to the grasshopper, mother dear, –
Like a green knight in a dazzling market-place, –
And listen now. Can you hear what I hear
Far out? Now and then the foam there curls
And stretches a white arm out like a girl's.

Fishes and gulls ring no bells. There cannot be
A chapel or church between here and Devon
With fishes or gulls ringing its bell, – hark. –
Somewhere under the sea or up in heaven.
'It's the bell, my son, out in the bay
On the buoy. It does sound sweet today.'

Sweeter I never heard, mother, no, not in all Wales.
I should like to be lying under that foam,
Dead, but able to hear the sound of the bell,
And certain that you would often come
And rest, listening happily.
I should be happy if that could be.

Letter to Eleanor Farjeon, 25 March 1915

The first lines of this letter encapsulate many features of Thomas's poetic composition process: the delight and speed with which he composed 'The Child on the Cliff', the unexpectedness with which his poems arrived, and his common experience of composing while in physical motion.

1915

29

My dear Eleanor,   Steep, Petersfield, 25 March 1915

Thank you. I have some more, too. It has perhaps become a really bad habit as I walk up the hill and I can sometimes hardly wait to light my fire. I am glad you find some things you like. I like the Child on the Cliff. It is a memory between one of my young brothers and myself which he reminded me of lately. He was most of the child and I have been truthful. I think I can expect some allowances for the 'strangeness' of the day. I wish I could cycle over at Easter but if I do go away I think it will be then and I should go west. Still, I might, and I am not *fixing* anything yet, and if I do the weather will intervene. I am still no walker except on smooth roads. But I hope you will be quite well by then. The weather has been tempting and tiring. We have done a lot of gardening, and never had the ground in better order so early. We expect Stanley this week end and shall look for news of you by him. I have a number of things to do in town, but I think I can see you on Wednesday or Thursday – next week that is: and I will write again when I know.

My mother had such a good letter from Mervyn about his detention and his whist playing with fellow prisoners. Now he is bored with Scott though.

Yours ever
Edward Thomas

I hope Eastaway gets the only rejected MSS at Fellows Rd; he gets them steadily.

But these things also
Steep, 18 March 1915

But these things also are Spring's –
On banks by the roadside the grass
Long-dead that is greyer now
Than all the Winter it was;

The shell of a little snail bleached
In the grass; chip of flint, and mite
Of chalk; and the small birds' dung
In splashes of purest white:

All the white things a man mistakes
For earliest violets
Who seeks through Winter's ruins
Something to pay Winter's debts,

While the North blows, and starling flocks
By chattering on and on
Keep their spirits up in the mist,
And Spring's here, Winter's not gone.

Letter to Edward Garnett, 17 March 1915

While clearly setting great store by Garnett's criticism, this letter also indicates Thomas's growing confidence in his poetry. His resistance of Garnett's criticism of what is 'petty in incident' is followed the next day by the composition of 'But these things also', a deliberate celebration of the 'petty'. He also refers in this letter to Garnett's comments on a number of his other poems.

My dear Garnett,   Steep, 17 March 1915

Your letter gave me a lot of pleasure this morning when few other things could because I had tired myself to death with two days cycling (to the sea and back) in this tempting and tiring weather – which is my reason for writing only a short note. I am fit for nothing at all really. I am glad to find you preferring certain things – like 'Old Man' and the 'Cuckoo' and 'Goodnight' – and sorry to find your preferring them to certain others like 'The Signpost'. But the great satisfaction is you obviously find them *like me*. I had fears lest I had got up in the air in this untried medium. So long as I haven't I am satisfied. Of course I must make mistakes and your preferences help me to see where they may lie, tho I shall risk some of them again – e.g. what you find petty in incident. Dimness and lack of concreteness I shall certainly do my best against. I hate them too much in others to tolerate them in myself – when I see them.

It was almost as pleasant to know you like Frost. The reviews he got here were one by Abercrombie in the *Nation*, one by Hueffer in the *Outlook*, and a number by me in the *New Weekly* etc. In America he got only an echo or two of these. He had been at American editors ten years in vain. But may I suggest it might damage him there if you rubbed the Americans' noses in their own dirt? I know he thought so. Most English reviewers were blinded by theories they had as to what poetry should look like. They did not see how true he was & how pure in his own style. I think 'The Hired Man,' 'The Wood Pile,' 'The Black Cottage' and one or two others – such as 'Home Burial' – masterpieces. I send his first book. Much of it is very early indeed. Look, however, at *Mowing* and *The Tuft of Flowers* (pp. 34 and 25). Hudson didn't return 'North of Boston,' or not to me. I will send him some of my verses.

The reason of my wire is that I am only sending out verses at present under a pseudonym, and have already done so to the *Nation*, *Times* and *English Review*. I don't want people to be confused by what they know or think of me already, although I know I shall also lose the advantage of some friendly prejudice. And I should be glad if you would not mention my verses to friends.

Frost is descended from early English (Devonshire) settlers, with a Scotch mother. He has farmed for some years and has gone back to farm. He has also been a teacher of English and pedagogy. – There are some of his latest verses in the last number of *Poetry and Drama*.

Yours ever
Edward Thomas

The New House

Now first, as I shut the door,
I was alone
In the new house; and the wind
Began to moan.

Old at once was the house,
And I was old;
My ears were teased with the dread
Of what was foretold,

Nights of storm, days of mist, without end;
Sad days when the sun
Shone in vain: old griefs, and griefs
Not yet begun.

All was foretold me; naught
Could I foresee;
But I learnt how the wind would sound
After these things should be.

Letter to Gordon Bottomley, 23 January 1913

This is one of a number of Thomas's letters to Bottomley emphasising the wind and rain around where he lived.

My dear Gordon,   Wick Green, 23 January 1913

This is a poor return for your letter, but better than a personal appearance just now, as I am feeling very old and useless, partly through wind and rain. But tell me whether any nights next week (save Tuesday & Wednesday) you would put me up. I shan't be in town except for ½ a day for nearly 3 weeks, but I would come over soon if I could stay a night.

I hope you will like Ellis. The catullus is an old friend & I send it to you because I have a poor but smaller version, & space is important in a tiny cottage such as we expect to move to in *June* or before.

I hope the wind & rain haven't been too much for you.
Emily didn't come over.
Goodbye
    Yours Ever
        Edward Thomas

Two Pewits
Steep, 24 March 1915, revised 4 May 1915

Under the after-sunset sky
Two pewits sport and cry,
More white than is the moon on high
Riding the dark surge silently;
More black than earth. Their cry
Is the one sound under the sky.
They alone move, now low, now high,
And merrily they cry
To the mischievous Spring sky,
Plunging earthward, tossing high,
Over the ghost who wonders why
So merrily they cry and fly,
Nor choose 'twixt earth and sky,
While the moon's quarter silently
Rides, and earth rests as silently.

Letter to Edward Garnett, early May 1915

The following lines are from an early draft of 'Two Pewits':

Two pewits sport and cry
Under the after-sunset sky,
Whiter than the moon on high
That rides the black surf in the sky,
Than the pool it is mirrored by,
The only light under the sky;

★★★

They care not for the sigh
Of the traveller wondering why
So merrily they cry and fly.
They choose not between earth and sky

A comparison between these lines and the finished poem shows Thomas responding to Garnett's criticism of 'divagations' in the following letter. He reorders the syntax and rewrites some lines to achieve greater clarity. In this letter, Thomas also discusses 'Lob'. Thomas's discussion of his preference for a looser 'unchiselled' line makes clear his emphasis on rhythm and sound when composing poetry. In an introduction to the 1927 *Selected Poems of Edward Thomas*, Garnett recalls his initial criticism of 'Lob' as 'a little breathless or rough'. This letter responds to that criticism.

My dear Garnett,   Steep, Petersfield, Monday, [early May 1915]

Your parcel came this morning. My best thanks for it, particularly for the letter & 'Frost'. I don't know yet how much I have to thank you for the 'Dials' & 'Poetry'. The article on Frost is absolutely right. I don't think you could have scored more than by insisting on his subtlety & truth & quoting the Hired Man, Home Burial & the Hundred Collars. And you have shown his nativeness + his Englishness very delicately & without a possibility of hurting anyone's feelings. There were two or three slips in the typescript that I took it on me to correct.

I am doubtful about the chiselling you advise. It would be the easiest thing in the world to clean it all up & trim it & have every line straightforward in sound & sense, but it would not really improve it. I think you read too much with the eye perhaps. If you *say* a couplet like

If they had mowed their dandelions & sold them fairly
they could have afforded gold –

I believe it is no longer awkward. The 'because' at the end of a line looks awkward if one is accustomed to an exaggerated stress on the rhyme word which I don't think is necessary. But I can't tell you how pleased I am that you like the long piece in the main & 'Pewits' too. I am going to try and be just about the lines you have marked in 'Pewits', though I am not sure whether you question the form of them or the 'divagations' of the idea, but probably the latter – if only I could hit upon some continuous form such as you suggest! I doubt if it will come by direct consideration. But I think perhaps intermingled prose & verse would add a difficulty. Even as it is I fancy the better passages in my prose lose by not really being happy in their places: verse might not lose so much, but the intervening prose would, unless of course one was very lucky. I shall cast about. I did half a fiction 12 months ago in one attempt but threw it up.

I am looking for a title for my proverb stories. If you like them I hope to have a title to suggest before they go before Duckworth. They are rather English, I fancy.

Scott James – I had almost forgotten to say – wrote and offered to recommend what I wrote on Rupert Brooke to the Bellman & I am just setting about it. The English Review also wants a short notice of R.B.

Next week I expect to be up on a final visit to the Museum before beginning to write about Marlborough. It is a wretched summer task. – I hope I shall see you again then.

Yours ever
Edward Thomas

Letter to Eleanor Farjeon, 5 May 1915

This letter refers both to Thomas's response to Garnett's criticism of 'Two Pewits' and to his poem 'April'.

My dear Eleanor   Steep, Petersfield, Tuesday,
                                   postmarked 5 May [1915]

I am afraid I may have to go up to town next week, on Tuesday or even Monday, to do another turn, I hope the last, at the Museum, and I thought I would let you know in case you might be able to come here before that or otherwise change your plans.

Did I tell you that I sent Monro a lot of verses in hopes he would make a book of them? Well, he won't. He doesn't like them at all. Nor does Ellis – he says their rhythm isn't obvious enough. I am busy consoling myself. I am not in the least influenced by such things: but one requires readjustment. I have stopped writing under the stress of Marlborough, though. This 'April' is the last. I send 'Pewits' because I have revised it. Garnett thought it was nearly very good indeed in its way, and I think perhaps it is clearer now, and it had to be as clear as glass.

Helen apologises for delaying with this 2/6.

Are you enjoying the rain and sun and everything with your whole self as I do in spite of Monro etc with some fraction of me?

Perhaps I shall go to Clifford's for one or 2 nights if he will have me and we can meet there.

Yours ever
Edward Thomas
P.S. [on flap of envelope] Just got your letter. So that is all right. Friday some time.

from *Wind and Mist*

Steep, 1 April 1915

'Sir, I know. I know. I have seen that house
Through mist look lovely as a castle in Spain,
And airier. I have thought: "'Twere happy there
To live." And I have laughed at that
Because I lived there then.' 'Extraordinary.'
'Yes, with my furniture and family
Still in it, I, knowing every nook of it
And loving none, and in fact hating it.'
'Dear me! How could that be? But pardon me.'
'No offence. Doubtless the house was not to blame,
But the eye watching from those windows saw,
Many a day, day after day, mist – mist
Like chaos surging back – and felt itself
Alone in all the world, marooned alone.
We lived in clouds, on a cliff's edge almost
(You see), and if clouds went, the visible earth
Lay too far off beneath and like a cloud.
I did not know it was the earth I loved
Until I tried to live there in the clouds
And the earth turned to cloud.'
                                 'You had a garden
Of flint and clay, too.' 'True; that was real enough.
The flint was the one crop that never failed.
The clay first broke my heart, and then my back;
And the back heals not. There were other things
Real, too. In that room at the gable a child
Was born while the wind chilled a summer dawn:
Never looked grey mind on a greyer one
Than when the child's cry broke above the groans.'
'I hope they were both spared.' 'They were. Oh yes.
But flint and clay and childbirth were too real
For this cloud castle. I had forgot the wind.
Pray do not let me get on to the wind.
You would not understand about the wind.
It is my subject, and compared with me
Those who have always lived on the firm ground
Are quite unreal in this matter of the wind.

Letters to Gordon Bottomley, 11 November 1906 and 26 August 1910

These letters not only contain the seeds of some of the lines of 'Wind and Mist', but show the two men's shared love of music and Thomas's habit of working in close collaboration with Bottomley on his prose works and anthologies.

Berryfield Cottage, Ashford, Petersfield,
My dear Gordon,   11 November 1906

This house & the country about it make the most beautiful place we ever lived in. We are now become people of whom passers by stop to think: How fortunate are they within those walls. I know it. I have thought the same as I came to the house & forgot it was my own.

But I am oppressed again by overmuch reviewing for *Chronicle World Bookman* & *Morning Post* & cannot find an hour to sink into myself or to write to you and Emily. You alone know how I felt at your words of praise & happiness after getting my book. All other copies ought to have been destroyed, for *World & Standard* have been saying what a cheery knowing companion I am for a day in the country & *The Academy* that I am affected & that in 'the heart of England' people do not speak so. I ought never to do colour books again. People can't believe there is anything in them at all.

Before I forget, 'New College Gardens' is to be found in *Songs of Love & Empire*. I didn't copy it out because I was very busy & I did not feel sure that you wanted it. Don't trouble about 'Goatfoot' now, I have copied it. A quarter of my anthology has gone to the printers. The songs are glorious – You should hear Campion's 'White Iope, blithe Helen & the rest', more religious than anything I know, & then 'Greensleeves' & 'Rio Grande' & Louis XIII's 'Amaryllis' & '*Orientis Partibus adventavit asinus*' (*La fête des fous*). It will be the best short collection in the world. I wish I thought as well of the poems.

How well you paint Bournemouth for me & the two windows & the cough.

To the Cymric enthusiast I only said that there was no Welsh original for 'Eluned' & that therefore he wd be disappointed because anyone can make a pseudo translation that suggests a noble original.

Goodbye Emily & Gordon. Helen sends her love with mine. I am yours ever
Edward Thomas

My dear Gordon,   Wick Green, 26 August 1910

I wish I were with you now or could come at once. I am back again
with the intolerable swishing of trees in the rain & wind which I have
had ever since I came here last Christmas. It makes me want to hear
music, & I have never enjoyed music anywhere as much as yours at
Well Knowe. However, I don't think I can come. I have just had a
couple of days on the Pilgrims Way in Kent & a couple with Conrad
but I was not well at least except when alone & out of doors. Now I
am expecting every day to go to Wales but am dependent on a trav-
elling companion. Since I finished the beastly book I have been
unable to work or rest, so I hope it will not be long. Proofs have begun
to arrive & perhaps I will send you the first batch now. It does look
horrible in small bits. Please send them back as quick as ever you can.
Or shall I only send you the page proofs. That would be kinder. Or
I will send you duplicates of the slips & use your suggestions in the
page proofs.

I am sending 'July'. It is one of those crude mixtures of experience
& invention which prove me no artist. Damn it. I am only just begin-
ning to discover it.

We haven't given the baby her names yet. We think of Olwen
Margaret Elizabeth or even Mevanwy (Myfanwy) Margaret Eliza-
beth, because Olwen is too like Bronwen. Helen is getting on very
well & sends her love to you & Emily. (This is vile paper).

I am too stupid to tell about Conrad, except that he looks some-
thing like Sir Richard Burton in the head, black hair, & moustache &
beard & a jutting out face, & pale thin lips extraordinarily mobile
among the black hair, flashing eyes and astonishing eyebrows, and a
way of throwing his head right back to laugh which he often does at
things which tickle him – such as Hueffer's 'harsh & oppressive' treat-
ment of the National Liberal Club porter. But I was uneasy with
Conrad – though he is very friendly to me – and kept saying things I
neither meant nor wished it to be supposed I meant. Alas! if only I
could live in solitude complete.

Ever yours Edward Thomas

from *Lob*

Steep, 3 and 4 April 1915

At hawthorn-time in Wiltshire travelling
In search of something chance would never bring,
An old man's face, by life and weather cut
And coloured, – rough, brown, sweet as any nut, –
A land face, sea-blue eyed, – hung in my mind
When I had left him many a mile behind.
All he said was: 'Nobody can't stop 'ee. It's
A footpath, right enough. You see those bits
Of mounds – that's where they opened up the barrows
Sixty years since, while I was scaring sparrows.
They thought as there was something to find there,
But couldn't find it, by digging, anywhere.'

To turn back then and seek him, where was the use?
There were three Manningfords, – Abbots, Bohun, and Bruce:
And whether Alton, not Manningford, it was
My memory could not decide, because
There was both Alton Barnes and Alton Priors.
All had their churches, graveyards, farms, and byres,
Lurking to one side up the paths and lanes,
Seldom well seen except by aeroplanes;
And when bells rang, or pigs squealed, or cocks crowed,
Then only heard. Ages ago the road
Approached. The people stood and looked and turned,
Nor asked it to come nearer, nor yet learned
To move out there and dwell in all men's dust.
And yet withal they shot the weathercock, just
Because 'twas he crowed out of tune, they said:
So now the copper weathercock is dead.
If they had reaped their dandelions and sold
Them fairly, they could have afforded gold.

Many years passed, and I went back again
Among those villages, and I looked for men
Who might have known my ancient. He himself
Had long been dead or laid upon the shelf,
I thought. One man I asked about him roared
At my description: ''Tis old Bottlesford

He means, Bill.' But another said: 'Of course,
It was Jack Button up at the White Horse.
He's dead, sir, these three years.' This lasted till
A girl proposed Walker of Walker's Hill,
'Old Adam Walker. Adam's Point you'll see
Marked on the maps.'

***

He is as English as this gate, these flowers, this mire.
And when at eight years old Lob-lie-by-the-fire
Came in my books, this was the man I saw.
He has been in England as long as dove and daw,
Calling the wild cherry tree the merry tree,
The rose campion Bridget-in-her-bravery;
And in a tender mood he, as I guess,
Christened one flower Live-in-idleness,
And while he walked from Exeter to Leeds
One April called all cuckoo-flowers Milkmaids.
From him old herbal Gerard learnt, as a boy,
To name wild clematis the Traveller's-joy.
Our blackbirds sang no English till his ear
Told him they called his Jan Toy "Pretty dear".

***

The man you saw, – Lob-lie-by-the-fire, Jack Cade,
Jack Smith, Jack Moon, poor Jack of every trade,
Young Jack, or old Jack, or Jack What-d'ye-call,
Jack-in-the-hedge, or Robin-run-by-the-wall,
Robin Hood, Ragged Robin, lazy Bob,
One of the lords of No Man's Land, good Lob, –
Although he was seen dying at Waterloo,
Hastings, Agincourt, and Sedgemoor, too, –
Lives yet.

from W.H. Davies, 'The Child and the Mariner', *Songs of Joy
and Others* **(London: A.C. Fifield, 1911), also in** *Georgian
Poetry 1911–12***, ed. Edward Marsh (London, Poetry Book-
shop, 1912)**

Thomas singles out Davies's long poem 'The Child and the

Mariner' for praise in his *Daily Chronicle* review of *Songs of Joy* on 30 January 1912. He calls it Davies's 'most perfect narrative descriptive poem in blank verse'. In his February 1912 *Bookman* review he also mentions the poem, describing it as abounding 'in gusto' and 'magic'.

> An old seafaring man was he; a rough
> Old man, but kind; and hairy, like the nut
> Full of sweet milk. All day on shore he watched
> The winds for sailors' wives, and told what ships
> Enjoyed fair weather, and what ships had storms;
> He watched the sky, and he could tell for sure
> What afternoons would follow stormy morns,
> If quiet nights would end wild afternoons.

Letter from Robert Frost to Edward Thomas, 17 April 1915 (extract)

Thomas had a habit of burning most of his papers when moving house, so this extract from a long letter Frost wrote to Thomas is one of only a small number of Frost's letters to Thomas that have survived.

Dear Edward   Littleton, New Hampshire, 17 April 1915

The goodness is in Lob. You are a poet or you are nothing. But you are not psychologist enough to know that no one not come at in just the right way will ever recognize you. *You* can't go to Garnett for yourself; *you* can't go to De la Mare. I told you and I keep telling you. But as long as your courage holds out you may as well go right ahead making a fool of yourself. All brave men are fools.

I like the first half of Lob best: it offers something more like action with the different people coming in and giving the tones of speech. But the long paragraph is a feat. I never saw anything like you for English.

★★★

Yours ever
R.F.

Letter to John Freeman, April 1915

This letter contains specific comments on 'Lob' that reveal Thomas's thinking about perception, connections and awareness of influences in his poetry. Thomas also comments on his poem 'The Barn and the Down'. See also Edward Garnett on 'Lob', p. 36.

My dear Freeman   13 Rusham Rd [April 1915]

Thank you very much. I am so glad you pointed out I'd missed a line: the couplet is 'Young Jack, or old Jack, or Jack What-d'ye-call, Jack-in-the-hedge, or Robin-run-by-the-wall, Robin Hood &c.' It connects the Jacks & the Bobs too.

What is the query about

'Seldom well seen except by aeroplanes'?

You can see these hamlets looking down in among the trees.

The other line is, I fear, echoed from a line in Adonais

He, as I guess,

Had looked on Nature's naked loveliness.

But isn't it alright, or mayn't Lob have been tender or have had a mood?

For goodness sake don't hesitate to say whatever occurs to you about the things, will you, so long as you have ink and you can't be lying out under the pear blossom. I hope you soon will be and Joy turning it into two kinds of poetry at once.

You were right about 'The Barn and the Down'. It ought to have been 2 plain verses *implying* all I've had to explain, I know. But I am not inclined to tinker.

It was a very real chill and all I could do was read down in the cottage for 4 days. I'm not used to chills and I was a nuisance. Now I'm better and reading at the Museum. Wolsley's 'Marlborough' has helped me. It is quite a good book and quotes by the way what he calls 'a burlesque of "The Happy Land", 1879', 'to the effect that a treaty is a promise made by a strong nation caught at a disadvantage which is to be put off at a convenient time'.

You are right also about Raleigh. He spent too much time learning to write better than he need.

You would like the country between Dymock and Redmarley d'Abitot: the red marl, the green grass, the larches and the Leadon, a beautiful stream there among woods.

Probably I shall see you in May when I next have to be up.

The 2nd of these 2 is the only thing I have by me.
Yours ever
Edward Thomas

Digging [1] ('Today I think')

Today I think
Only with scents, – scents dead leaves yield,
And bracken, and wild carrot's seed,
And the square mustard field;

Odours that rise
When the spade wounds the roots of tree,
Rose, currant, raspberry, or goutweed,
Rhubarb or celery;

The smoke's smell, too,
Flowing from where a bonfire burns
The dead, the waste, the dangerous,
And all to sweetness turns.

It is enough
To smell, to crumble the dark earth,
While the robin sings over again
Sad songs of Autumn mirth.

Letter to Gordon Bottomley, 10 November 1902

In this letter Thomas's discussion of Bottomley's one act play
The Crier by Night reveals Thomas's awareness of the difficulty
of writing on scent.

To the writer of *The Crier by Night*   Rose Acre,
Greetings and congratulations –   10 November 1902

I read the play as I said I would, on the Saturday before last at an inn
on the Pilgrim's Road, and I have just read it again, not so much to
look for beauties or faults as to renew the unbroken wave of pleasure
which it gave me at first. For me, at any rate, the play is a delicate
experience and I don't want to criticize it. I said it gave an *unbroken*
wave etc, because it seemed to me to have perfect unity; that is a great
thing. As to the nature of the impression it made, I find it hard to
speak. There are a few books or passages in books – in W.B. Yeats,
in Keats, in *The Roadmender*, in *The Opium Eater* & *Religio Medici* &

one or two more – which quite overcome my intelligence, because (I think) I am so much in sympathy with them that they seem to belong to my own experience; in some cases, I even feel, I hope not impudently, 'I ought to have written that myself!' That is how I felt when I put down your book. The story, the air of the thing, above all the rhythm, made an atmosphere that I lived in more freely than I can often do. It is magical; your Muse is the one that visits Yeats. In two places only I think the Muse was ungenerous to you (or you did not listen to Her). I mean in the lyrics. The first one contains several lines that are exquisite in sound, but I cannot justify your use of 'hear' in this line –

'The scent of the mead at the harping I shall not hear again.'

The three verses don't seem to me clear enough. You are fantastic in other places, but in these lyrics I see an effort at being fantastic which is invisible elsewhere. Thus in the line –

'My bare cry shivers along the shiny rushes of the drowned lake.'

I know exactly what you mean, but I think the expression does not properly clothe the fancy. Still it is a terribly difficult thing to express; it is a fancy that would come to anybody else almost as elusively and untranslatably as for example a scent. That is your danger; you hover continually on the verge of what is probably inexpressible. Your success is all the more brilliant. I have one quibble: you use the word 'imaged' too often, & where you use the word twice in successive lines you are obscure... Where did you get the cry 'Ohohey' from? I quite frightened myself by repeating it on a dark road.

You know I spoke about certain books as *feeding* me? Yours is one. It sets my brain on fire. I could write an essay on it or 'after' it, & someday I hope I shall; but I am still busy reviewing, & there are many things I have to postpone. So this note is merely a greeting & congratulation. Have you a copy of *White Nights* I could see? I think Helen has a letter for you. She sends her love with mine.

Edward Thomas

Letters to W.H. Hudson and J.W. Haines, June 1914 and 4 January 1915 (extracts)

The June 1914 extract from the Hudson letter, quoted in the *London Mercury*, 10 August 1920, shows Thomas's great interest in the scents of nature, also reflected in 'Digging [I]'. A similar interest in scent is expressed in the January 1915 extract from a letter to Haines, which reiterates the importance of Geof-

frey Winthrop Young's 'Stone Chat' to Thomas at this time, a
poem that also emphasises the senses (see p. 68).

[To W. H. Hudson]   June 1914

I have been wanting, especially when I was up near Kendal, to ask
you about a scent I notice every year, and used to think came from
young shoots of some pine or yew. But now I hardly think it is from
any leaf or flower. It has something of the scent of young yew shoots,
but it is sweeter, almost as if it had been mixed with honeysuckle. I
have noticed it where there were no flowers, but only a mixture of
hazel and scrub, oak and grasses, and perhaps bracken. Are there
sweet-scented beetles as well as nauseous ones?

[To J.W. Haines]   Steep, 4 January 1915

Many thanks for your letter. I have got a lot of time to reply to it being
in bed with a sprained ankle, but not much ability. Only I thought of
you this morning when the children brought in some winter
heliotrope from near by. You know the dull thing with sleepy trails
that look as if they ought to be leaves, and flowers that look like cotton
tassels. But the smell suggests lilac as well as heliotrope, and is a very
curious treasure for January 4th. This can't be a *reply* to your letter
either because yours is over the other side of the room and I am alone
in the house for the afternoon.

I wonder how you liked *The Stonechat* in Geoffrey Young's book,
if at all. I have only just ventured to write again to Hudson after his
sarcastic remark that Young had never heard a stonechat sing (which
is the root of his dislike – I having put him on the scent of an imper-
fect naturalist by mentioning the 'wetstone' before sending the poem
– he immediately anticipated a man who could mistake a wheatear
for a stonechat).

I have a devil of a job before me. I have undertaken to say some-
thing about what people mean when they speak of 'England'
nowadays, and now I can't get about to draw them. Point-blank ques-
tions aren't much use, but you won't mind my *asking* – as I shan't
mind your not answering – whether you do instinctively (and without
setting yourself to think about it) have some place or person or event
or speech in your mind when you use the word or when it occurs to
you, and especially since the beginning of the war. *The Times Supple-
ment* had an article about England being Devon moors, Cumberland
hills, Surrey commons, Welsh song, etc. But it was too rhetorical, and

didn't convey precisely what it was *to the writer* (who happens to know nothing of Welsh song and Cumberland hills). I hope this question won't put you into the frame of mind of a school-boy asked for an essay because (1) I should be sorry to afflict you and (2) it wouldn't produce what I want probably.

Home [2] ('Often I had gone this way before')

Steep, 17 April 1915

Often I had gone this way before:
But now it seemed I never could be
And never had been anywhere else;
'Twas home; one nationality
We had, I and the birds that sang,
One memory.

They welcomed me. I had come back
That eve somehow from somewhere far:
The April mist, the chill, the calm,
Meant the same thing familiar
And pleasant to us, and strange too,
Yet with no bar.

The thrush on the oak top in the lane
Sang his last song, or last but one;
And as he ended, on the elm
Another had but just begun
His last; they knew no more than I
The day was done.

Then past his dark white cottage front
A labourer went along, his tread
Slow, half with weariness half with ease;
And, through the silence, from his shed
The sound of sawing rounded all
That silence said.

Walter de la Mare, 'Sorcery', *Poems* (London: John Murray, 1906)

Thomas reviewed de la Mare's *Poems* in the *Daily Chronicle*, 9 November 1906, and the December 1910 *English Review*. The scene described in de la Mare's 'Sorcery' is recast in 'Home [2]', shorn of its pantheism, with the labourer's blade now carving out the end of the poem.

'What voice is that I hear
Crying across the pool?'
'It is the voice of Pan you hear,
Crying his sorceries shrill and clear,
In the twilight dim and cool.'

'What song is it he sings,
Echoing from afar;
While the sweet swallow bends her wings,
Filling the air with twitterings,
Beneath the brightening star?'

The woodman answered me,
His faggot on his back: –
'Seek not the face of Pan to see;
Flee from his clear note summoning thee
To darkness deep and black!

'He dwells in the thickest shade,
Piping his notes forlorn
Of sorrow never to be allayed;
Turn from his coverts sad
Of twilight unto morn!'

The woodman passed away
Along the forest path;
His axe shone keen and grey
In the last beams of day:
And all was still as death: –

Only Pan singing sweet
Out of Earth's fragrant shade;
I dreamed his eyes to meet,
And found but shadow laid
Before my tired feet.

Comes no more dawn to me,
Nor bird of open skies.
Only his woods' deep gloom I see
Till, at the end of all, shall rise,
Afar and tranquilly,
Death's stretching sea.

1915

Letters to Eleanor Farjeon, 5 and 12 November 1913

Written a year and a half before 'Home [2]', these letters record
Thomas's immersion at this time in the life and poems of Keats,
and his simultaneous awareness of thrush song and of the sound
of builders at work. These elements seem to be recombined in
'Home [2]', indicating Thomas's habit of drawing on earlier
memories when composing.

My dear Eleanor, [Selsfield House], 5 November [1913]

Thank you for the stationery. I know. I am sorry I couldn't begin to
use it sooner. But I have not found life any better tho it is simpler, &
I have been working all day, really hard, as hard as one can in my state
of mind, & this very day I have begun to write an abridgement of what
I have been reading about Keats' life & character. It is difficult & slow
& unrewarding & my head's thick with it & I am furthermore anxious
as to whether I shall do anything but abridge – e.g. say something
about the poems that I really think. However, it is begun. A thrush
sings every hour of the daylight as I work, from 6.30 to 5: also men
hammer & saw, repairing Ellis' dilapidations. So you will agree that
Keats is better off than I, though he couldn't buy Donald's photo-
graph or even want to. – Mrs Cox, mother of Theresa, Honor &
Barbara Cox, of Sizewell was here for the week-end. – What an
absurd remark. This is to say that I hope you are well & see Clifford
& Godwin & other blessed inhabitants of the earth.
        Yours ever
        Edward Thomas

My dear Eleanor, Petersfield, 12 November [1913]

I am glad you began to like the book, & hope others will do so. My
next best appreciators are the Australians. They have been ordering
2000 copies of my 'Celtic Stories' for their schools. I didn't think they
(the Colonials) had any virtues.
        I hope Clifford & Olga will come through all right & get to peace.
I entirely agree with you without hesitation, because I know that
Daphne would be no better & Clifford the worse for making any
attempt to abide by the letter of their marriage, especially as there is
money enough to keep them separately, & as Clifford is called away
so decidedly. Please give Clifford my love & blessing. I may be in town
on Monday next, & would like to go over there & see him, but not if
he is still busy with his troubles. Could we both go there at tea-time?

Edward Thomas's Poets

You are used now to these skimming letters. I am still deep in Keats, & getting on as well as I could have hoped & better than I expected, only by filling my days & latterly my nights with it, to the neglect of everything else.

My Times article is not to be printed. It overlapped with another already done, was not (they say through no fault of mine) what they wanted, so they got another man to do it in a hurry & have sent me another book, & I don't know yet if the review of that will please them any better.

I didn't complain of the thrush! He is a most noble bird, & sings in the wildest & darkest dawns eternally as if he were in a poem & not born for death at all like other thrushes & me.

Goodbye
Edward Thomas

April

Steep, 2 May 1915

The sweetest thing, I thought
At one time, between earth and heaven
Was the first smile
When mist has been forgiven
And the sun has stolen out,
Peered, and resolved to shine at seven
On dabbled lengthening grasses,
Thick primroses and early leaves uneven,
When earth's breath, warm and humid, far surpasses
The richest oven's, and loudly rings 'cuckoo'
And sharply the nightingale's 'tsoo, troo, tsoo, troo';
To say 'God bless it' was all that I could do.

But now I know one sweeter
By far since the day Emily
Turned weeping back
To me, still happy me,
To ask forgiveness, –
Yet smiled with half a certainty
To be forgiven, – for what
She had never done; I knew not what it might be,
Nor could she tell me, having now forgot,
By rapture carried with me past all care
As to an isle in April lovelier
Than April's self. 'God bless you' I said to her.

Letter to Robert Frost, 3 May 1915

Near the end of this letter Thomas paraphrases parts of 'April'.
Thomas's own 'nothing to say' acts as an implicit criticism of
Rupert Brooke's 'eloquence'. For more on Thomas's view of
Brooke at this time, see his letter to J.W. Haines on 5 May 1915
and to Frost on 13 June 1915 (pp. 136, 137).

My dear Robert   Steep, Monday 3 May 1915

I got a letter from you on Friday, the one I have been gladdest to yet,
& not only because you said you liked Lob. I was glad to hear of your

going to Stowe 'tomorrow'. You are enjoying this period, but it is silly of me to tell you so. If you aren't you ought to be, because you are not writing about Marlborough. But we have one piece of luck. Two pairs of nightingales have come to us. One sings in our back hedge nearly all day & night. My only regret when I first heard it was that you hadn't stayed another Spring & heard it too. I hope the gods don't think I'm the sort of poet who will be content with a nightingale, though. You don't think they could have made that mistake do you? What does it mean? I get quite annoyed with people complaining of the weather as soon as it greys a little. Am I really ripe for being all sound content, or what? 2nd piece of luck (still embryonic) is that Scott-James has some connections with an American literary journal called The Bellman & is recommending them things by me, beginning with a remark on Rupert Brooke. You heard perhaps that he died on April 23rd of sunstroke on the way to the Dardenelles? All the papers are full of his 'beauty' & an eloquent last sonnet beginning 'If I should die.' He was eloquent. Men never spoke ill of him.

But you have some poems by you fit to send, haven't you? These editors mustn't go sour with waiting.

I find I can't write. Re-reading Rupert Brooke & putting a few things together about him have rather messed me up & there's Marlborough behind & Marlborough before. I shall have to go up to London for the last time next week – for the last bout at the Museum, I mean. Bronwen is now at school again. I shall take Baba up & leave Helen to contrive some spring cleaning. I tell you – I should like another April week in Gloucestershire with you like that one last year. You are the only person I can be idle with. That's natural history, not eloquence. If you were there I might even break away from the Duke for 3 days, but it would be hard.

Are the children at school now? Or are you still 'neglecting' them? God bless them all. By the way, there was a beautiful return of sun yesterday after a misty moisty morning, & everything smelt wet & warm & cuckoos called, & I found myself with nothing to say but 'God bless it'. I laughed a little as I came over the field, thinking about the 'it' in 'God bless it'.

Yours & Elinor's ever
Edward Thomas

Don't send back that parson's letter and of course keep the poems. (I haven't quite stopped even yet.)

P.S. Here is Ellis very elderly and masterly about my verses, not finding one to say he likes, but seeing the 'elements of poetry'. The rhythm is too rough and not obvious enough. He wants to talk them over. I don't. Well, I feel sure I'm old enough not to know better, though I don't profess to know how good or bad it may be.

Fifty Faggots

British Museum, 13 May 1915

There they stand, on their ends, the fifty faggots
That once were underwood of hazel and ash
In Jenny Pinks's Copse. Now, by the hedge
Close packed, they make a thicket fancy alone
Can creep through with the mouse and wren. Next Spring
A blackbird or a robin will nest there,
Accustomed to them, thinking they will remain
Whatever is for ever to a bird:
This Spring it is too late; the swift has come.
'Twas a hot day for carrying them up:
Better they will never warm me, though they must
Light several Winters' fires. Before they are done
The war will have ended, many other things
Have ended, maybe, that I can no more
Foresee or more control than robin and wren.

Robert Frost, 'The Wood-Pile', *North of Boston* (London: David Nutt, 1914)

Thomas quotes from this poem in his reviews of *North of Boston* in the *Daily News* (22 July 1914) and the *New Weekly* (8 August 1914). He calls it a 'masterpiece' in the August 1914 *English Review*.

Out walking in the frozen swamp one grey day,
I paused and said, 'I will turn back from here.
No, I will go on farther – and we shall see.'
The hard snow held me, save where now and then
One foot went down. The view was all in lines
Straight up and down of tall slim trees
Too much alike to mark or name a place by
So as to say for certain I was here
Or somewhere else: I was just far from home.
A small bird flew before me. He was careful
To put a tree between us when he lighted,
And say no word to tell me who he was
Who was so foolish as to think what *he* thought.
He thought that I was after him for a feather –

The white one in his tail; like one who takes
Everything said as personal to himself.
One flight out sideways would have undeceived him.
And then there was a pile of wood for which
I forgot him and let his little fear
Carry him off the way I might have gone,
Without so much as wishing him good-night.
He went behind it to make his last stand.
It was a cord of maple, cut and split
And piled – and measured, four by four by eight.
And not another like it could I see.
No runner tracks in this year's snow looped near it.
And it was older sure than this year's cutting,
Or even last year's or the year's before.
The wood was grey and the bark warping off it
And the pile somewhat sunken. Clematis
Had wound strings round and round it like a bundle.
What held it though on one side was a tree
Still growing, and on one a stake and prop,
These latter about to fall. I thought that only
Someone who lived in turning to fresh tasks
Could so forget his handiwork on which
He spent himself, the labour of his axe,
And leave it there far from a useful fireplace
To warm the frozen swamp as best it could
With the slow smokeless burning of decay.

Letters to Robert Frost, 15 May 1915 and 9 September 1916 (extract)

The letter of 15 May 1915 includes paraphrases of Gordon
Bottomley's, Vivian Locke Ellis's and Harold Monro's criticism
of Thomas's poetry, and implies that for Thomas the concep-
tion and execution of his poetry occurred simultaneously. The
extract from the 9 September 1916 letter reveals the autobio-
graphical base of 'Fifty Faggots', and once again implies the lack
of *conscious attention* on Thomas's part when writing his poetry
(as opposed to focusing on his work). The reference to 'rain &
wind' could refer to Thomas's 'The Source'.

My dear Robert   London, Saturday, 15 May [1915]

The Lusitania seems to increase the distance between us, unless I am really suffering just from a week in London. This is the end of I hope my last week's reading for 'Marlborough'. Helen is at home Spring cleaning. I go back on Monday or Tuesday with Baba to begin writing. I have seen a few people at meals, Scott-James among others. He is English advisor to the Minneapolis 'Bellman', a pretty good weekly that may be persuaded by him to print me. The only news is that Hodgson is now in the anti-aircraft squadron patrolling the East coast chiefly with special guns mounted on motor cars. He will be happier.

One of my reliefs in this week's work was to write these lines founded on carrying up 50 bunts (short faggots of thin & thick brushwood mixed) & putting them against our hedge:

> There they stand, on their ends, the fifty bunts
> That once were underwood of hazel & ash
> In Jenny Pinks's Copse. Now by the hedge
> Close packed they make a thicket fancy alone
> Can creep through with the mouse & wren. Next Spring
> A blackbird or a robin will nest there,
> Accustomed to them, thinking they will remain
> Whatever is for ever to a bird.
> This Spring it is too late: – the swifts are here:
> 'Twas a hot day for carrying them up.
> Better they will never warm me, though they must
> Light several winters' fires. Before they are done
> The war will have ended, many other things
> Have ended that I know not more about
> And care not less for than robin or wren.

Are they *north* of Boston only? I must try them on Bottomley. I sent him a small batch that didn't include 'Lob' & he put whatever may have been his feeling about them into a rather polite friendly form, concluding: 'My only real & serious criticism is that you tend to use words in the spirit of the prose-writer, respecting first their utility & the syntax which everyday use requires them to observe. When formal rhythm & metre are allowed to regulate the use of language, utilitarian purposes are abandoned; language is thus freed to move according to its own interior purposes of cadence or pattern or suggestion, ...'. There is something in it; but nothing to learn. I can't *try* to write unlike a prose-writer or *try* to get freer from straightforward constructions. I am a little consoled too because what he liked most (& thought best) was a passage where I had allowed 'rain & wind' to come in 3 or 4 times or more usually at the end of a line, in about twice the number of blank verse lines.

I have now gone the round of pretty well all the verse-writers I know. Ellis was kind enough to find mine 'eminently the stuff of which poetry is made' &c. Thinking he might make a book of them I did at last send a selection to Monro. He didn't like it. He muttered something about conception & execution as if they were different things. But I had requested him not to trouble to give reasons why he liked or didn't like them.

If you have a farm by now these remarks will easily sink into perspective. But I am thinned out by all this reading & smoking.

My love to you all,
Yours ever
Edward Thomas

My dear Robert,   13 Rusham Rd, 9 September 1916

***

But I don't want money. Didn't I tell you the government had been persuaded to grant me £300? They would not give me a pension. That £300 might last till the end of the war. But those 50 faggots didn't. We took to cooking with them in the Summer out of doors & that spoilt my verses on the subject so far as they were a prophecy. It is no use me saying how much I wish I were destined to come & live at your farm. You know I think of it often. But of course the future is less explorable than usual, and I don't take it (the future) quite seriously. I find myself thinking as if there wasn't going to be no future. This isn't perversity. I say I find myself doing so. On the other hand it may be I am just as wrong as when I wrote about those 50 faggots. I thought then that one simply had to wait a very long time. I wonder if it is pleasanter to be Rupert Brookeish. Anyhow it is impossible, & I suppose I enjoy this frame of mind as much as I can enjoy anything (beyond my dinner) at present.

Monday the 11th
This frame of mind is lasting too long. The fact is – my cold is worse & I am sick at not being really equal to my work. Once I get into the country I shall be all right.

I don't believe I can do much yet at 'The Old Cloak'. You can't imagine the degree of my disinclination for books. Sometimes I say I will read Shakespeare's Sonnets again & I do, or half do, but never more than that I should love to do it with you. I thought of what love poems would go in – could Burns's 'Whistle & I'll come to ye, my lad?' There are the songs in the very earliest Elizabethan dramatists. There's a deal of Chaucer, Shakespeare, Cowper, Wordsworth & the ballads: some Crabbe; one poem apiece out of Prior & several minor 18th century people: a few of Blake's. But I daren't begin to look at books. I must keep all my *conscious attention* for my work.

***

Yours ever
Edward Thomas

Sedge-Warblers

Steep, 23–4 May 1915

This beauty makes me dream there was a time
Long past and irrecoverable, a clime
Where river of such radiance racing clear
Through buttercup and kingcup bright as brass
But gentle, nourishing the meadowgrass
That leans and scurries in the wind, would bear
Another beauty, divine and feminine,
Child of the sun, whose happy soul unstained
Could love all day, and never hate or tire,
Lover of mortal or immortal kin.

And yet rid of this dream, ere I had drained
Its poison, quieted was my desire
So that I only looked into the water
And hearkened, while it combed the dark-green hair
And shook the millions of the blossoms white
Of water crowfoot, and curdled in one sheet
The flowers fallen from the chestnuts in the park
Far off. The sedgewarblers that hung so light
On willow twigs, sang longer than any lark,
Quick, shrill or grating, a song to match the heat
Of the strong sun, nor less the water's cool
Gushing through narrows, swirling in the pool.
Their song that lacks all words, all melody,
All sweetness almost, was dearer now to me
Than sweetest voice that sings in tune sweet words:
This was the best of May, the small brown birds
Wisely reiterating endlessly
What no man learnt yet, in or out of school.

Letter to Eleanor Farjeon, 8 June 1915

My dear Eleanor   Monday, postmarked 8 June 1915

Thank you again, but I didn't want you to trouble with Faggots. I am
glad you liked the Sedgewarblers. Of course if I could really bring
things pure and clear through verse into people's heads it would be a
great thing. I rather fancy you doubt if it would necessarily be poetry.

Well, I don't know either and I am not sure that I care. I am not trying to do anything in particular but only hoping that at last I have stepped into the nearest approach I ever made yet to self-expression. I expect that line ending in 'hair' was to rhyme with 2 lines higher up – As to the 3-word line I thought it was right somehow, but there was nothing intentional about it. But I am up to the neck in Marlborough. 7 hours writing every day, and the rest reading in preparation and going over notes. I am afraid I ought to be on the top of Ararat or somewhere. I am getting a nuisance to mankind with my concentration on the silly thing. However I am rather thinking of finishing or all but finishing on Saturday week, and then cycling with a man whose holiday falls then up to Gloster and even Coventry – through Avebury maybe. Then it looks as if I must decide something as no other work awaits me except doing some tales of the English traveller-explorers which would be practically paraphrasing, which I do loathe. I have got no farther in thoughts of America. No, I don't think I would even so have asked you to let me have that money. I want to stave off dependence except in little odds and ends – very many they have long been – till I can do no more. It is wretched to be willing to work, to think I know what I can do, and yet not to be sure of £150 a year. I don't imagine I *deserve* anything but I am afraid I instinctively act as if I did and don't make the efforts other people seem to think I could make. I must read 'Self-help'. The point is I can do my own work without being told or directed, but I wait or can't do anything else unless I am not told. If anybody said You go and join the Royal Garrison Artillery and they will give you a commission, I believe I should go next month.

Frost's address is still Littleton. No letter from him this week.

The nightingales only make little remarks to themselves as they go about getting food I suppose for their young.

Now I must go.

Yours ever

Edward Thomas

I built myself a house of glass

I built myself a house of glass:
It took me years to make it:
And I was proud. But now, alas,
Would God someone would break it.

But it looks too magnificent.
No neighbour casts a stone
From where he dwells, in tenement
Or palace of glass, alone.

Letter to Eleanor Farjeon, 5 April 1915

My dear Eleanor   Monday, postmarked 5 April 1915

Baba and I thank you for the egg which we killed between us. I must try sending you glass or may be I am immune as living in a glass house and throwing stones. Now I have got to work. I have practically accepted the filthy job – a book on the Duke of Marlborough to be done in haste. I am coming up at once to the Museum. One day I will have tea with you if you will have tea with me, say on *Thursday* at 4.30. I could meet you anywhere between the Reading Room and the nearest Express Dairy. This seems to knock all travel on the head this spring.

Did I tell you I removed the Old Balaban and the Yost and I are friends for ever!

Yours ever
Edward Thomas

Letter to Edward Garnett, 24 June 1915

'I Built myself a House of Glass' was composed while Thomas was staying with J.W. Haines in Gloucester, during which time they cycled to May Hill, near Glass House hill. His concerns about his shyness and self-consciousness in this letter are reflected in the poem.

My dear Garnett   c/o J.W. Haines, Hillview Road,
                                   Hucclecote, Glos, 24 June 1915

Thank you for writing at once. I got your letter when I arrived here
from Malmesbury last night. But I can't really answer till I have been
able to think a little more. I can only say now that at first sight you
seem to ask me to try to turn over a new leaf and be someone else. I
can't help dreading people both in anticipation and when I am among
them and my only way of holding my own is the instinctive one of
turning on what you call coldness and a superior manner. That is why
I hesitated about America. I felt sure that unless I could make a friend
or two I could do no good. – Nor do I think that any amount of
distress could turn me into a lecturer. It would weary you if I tried to
explain: I don't justify. – But these are first thoughts and I am tired
rather.

As to the Civil List, will you ask Hudson? I believe others might
speak to Lloyd George. I hate the idea of *urging* it, but I am urged
and I know that somehow or another I must find some sort of safety
however low. Anything rather than a continuation of the insecurity
of the last three years. Anything (I must add before you say it) rather
than make a bold bid. Anything (I suppose) rather than be inde-
pendent.

However I think I shall go over to America in a couple of months
and see what I can make myself do.

I shall write again. I stay here till Saturday or Sunday, then go on
to Bablake School Coventry and so back home, I should think
through Oxford.

I have had four marvellous fine long days on end through
Salisbury Shaftesbury Avebury Wootton Bassett Tetbury and
Malmesbury here.

Yours ever

Edward Thomas

I hope I shall see you before you go. Good luck to David.

Words

'Hucclecote – on the road from Gloster to Coventry',
26-8 June 1915

Out of us all
That make rhymes,
Will you choose
Sometimes –
As the winds use
A crack in a wall
Or a drain,
Their joy or their pain
To whistle through –
Choose me,
You English words?

I know you:
You are light as dreams,
Tough as oak,
Precious as gold,
As poppies and corn,
Or an old cloak:
Sweet as our birds
To the ear,
As the burnet rose
In the heat
Of Midsummer:
Strange as the races
Of dead and unborn:
Strange and sweet
Equally,
And familiar,
To the eye,
As the dearest faces
That a man knows,
And as lost homes are:
But though older far
Than oldest yew, –
As our hills are, old, –
Worn new
Again and again;

Young as our streams
After rain:
And as dear
As the earth which you prove
That we love.

Make me content
With some sweetness
From Wales
Whose nightingales
Have no wings, –
From Wiltshire and Kent
And Herefordshire,
And the villages there, –
From the names, and the things
No less.

Let me sometimes dance
With you,
Or climb
Or stand perchance
In ecstasy,
Fixed and free
In a rhyme,
As poets do.

Edward Thomas's pseudo-translation 'Eluned', *Beautiful Wales* **(London: Black, 1905)**

The second verse of 'Eluned' is echoed in the second verse of 'Words'.

She is dead, Eluned,
Whom the young men and the old men
And the old women and even the young women
Came to the gates in the village
To see, because she walked as beautifully as a heifer.

She is dead, Eluned,
Who sang the new songs
And the old; and made the new

Seem old, and the old
As if they were just born and she had christened them.

She is dead, Eluned,
Whom I admired and loved,
When she was gathering red apples,
When she was making bread and cakes,
When she was smiling to herself and not thinking of me.

She is dead, Eluned,
Who was part of Spring,
And of blue Summer and red Autumn,
And made Winter beloved:
She is dead, and these things come not again.

Geoffrey Winthrop Young, 'Stone Chat' *Freedom: Poems* (London: Smith, Elder & Co., 1914)

In a letter of 26 November 1914 to W.H. Hudson, Thomas praised 'Stone Chat' as being 'one of the best of all pure bird poems, the bird on a wet stone pure and simple up on a heath'. The rhythm and tone of the poem bear some similarities to 'Words'.

Out of the mist,
little friend, little mate,
the wet white mist on the wet flat stone,
with the rain around you,
you frisk with a flirt
of your brisk little wing
and a pert
little twist of your beak to sing; –
– cheek! – cheek! –
a perk, and a hop
to my bleak wet stone;
– found you! – found you –
out of the mist on the flat hill-top
in the wind, and alone.

What a warm black strap
for a warm orange coat!

Edward Thomas's Poets

and your throat –
chack, chack –
what a note – what a note!
the sharp wet snap of a pebble on slate:
little friend, mayhap –
– chack! – he is gone:
but again, from a stone,
from a wet stone, flat stone,
– chat! –chat! –
THAT
is the chirp of my mate,
the stone-chat, stone-chat,
out in the mist,
out in the mist and the rain,
happy alone,
        the jolly little chap.

Letters to Gordon Bottomley, Robert Frost and Eleanor Farjeon, 18 June 1915, 28 June 1915 and 29 June 1915

These letters trace the preoccupations in Thomas's mind and his physical circumstances at the time of the composition of 'Words', which took place during a cycle ride with Haines around May Hill in Gloucestershire; at Haines's house; and, the following day, on a cycle ride to Coventry. In the 18 June 1915 letter to Bottomley, Thomas continues a previous epistolary discussion about his and Frost's poetry, the last paragraph indicating the issues then in the forefront of Thomas's mind. The letter to Frost, written just after the composition of 'Words' and including an early version of the poem, reveals details of the physical circumstances in which the poem was written. The letter to Eleanor Farjeon makes clear the disjointed nature of that composition process, on separate scraps of paper.

My dear Gordon,   Steep, 18 June 1915

I am afraid I let my irritation at Sturge Moore's criticism of Frost run over into what I said about your criticism of me. I mean I think it may have appeared so. But really it did not. I could not help, of course, some uncertainty as to the extent of your qualification when you advised me to 'stick to' my material. But I was pleased entirely with your liking of 'Lob' and everything you said was either pleasant or interesting. Not that what was interesting was unpleasant & what was pleasant uninteresting. No it was a letter I was altogether glad to have apart from the quotation from S.M. & even that gave me the satisfaction of knowing that if a man like S.M. misses Frost so completely I can stand being missed myself in turn. There. I do hope I have undone anything I did that I ought not to have done in my letter on Wednesday.

Now I am going to cycle & think of man & life & human nature & decide between enlisting or going to America before I enlist. Those are the alternatives unless something else turns up out of the dark.

Yours ever
Edward Thomas

My dear Robert   Coventry, Monday, 28 June 1915

I have just come on here from Haines's by cycle. I had 3 days there cycling about & talking of you. One day at Gloster station we met the Abercrombies just off to London. He was very well & lively, but she is changed & looks done. We went to May Hill from another side but not to the crest or any of the points we touched. I began to versify again but now I have had a smack in the face from the publishers of my Marlborough who say it is short of the stipulated length. Hodson here promises to take Mervyn at his school for a year to prepare for going into engineering works in the town & I hope it will come off. He also indefinitely suggests me coming here as English master. But it is only temporary – while another man is at the front – and in any case I am not sure I ought to let it interfere with my idea of coming out to Boston & north of Boston, though if I *could* do it I should have broken some ice.

I've had extraordinary luck in weather, all fine days when I was riding, & this is the 8th day, & I began (as I thought) at the end of a very long period of dry heat. It is just like last year in fact.

Haines & I got on well enough, tho he is restless out of doors with his coffer for plants, his dislike of thunder (we had a storm), and his punctuality for meals. He doesn't fertilise. But he is a good soul, & he only read one of his poems, a thing about a number of different flowers in the Lake District, incredibly undistinguished. I doubt if a botanist can write tolerably about flowers tho a sailor can about the sea.

De la Mare has got £100 a year now from the Civil List, & he was making £400 at least. I suppose his illness was the excuse. I was annoyed especially as I am told I have no chance myself as being too young & not as well known as many others who will be applying. Let me admit also that I felt they might have let me sign the petition as I have probably reviewed him more than anyone else. That is frank. The news spoilt one of my days' cycling. If he didn't give me such opulent dinners when I went there I should mind less.

I send you the rhymes I made at Haines's & on my way here yesterday.

Helen sent me on Elinor's letter from Franconia & I was very glad to see it. You have had some luck. I wish I was there with you all.

Haines showed me a photograph of you. At first I wished I had one. But now I think I have a better one.

Yours ever
Edward Thomas

My dear Eleanor   Coventry, postmarked 29 June 1915

I have altered this, or rather (chiefly) put in two lines that got left out owing to the scraps I wrote on as I travelled. I hope you have had no more midnight telephone.

We have got lovely rain that looks like preventing my ride.

That beastly Marlborough is worse than any weather.

Yours ever
Edward Thomas

Letter to Gordon Bottomley, 30 June 1915

In this letter, which included a copy of 'Words', Thomas continues his discussion of Frost's theory of poetry. This discussion clearly informed 'Words', itself a meditation on the composition process.

My dear Gordon,   Coventry (till tomorrow then home),
                                              30 June 1915

Your letter followed me about on a cycling journey up thro Gloster here – a premature holiday to get rid of the effect of *Marlborough*, for they now tell me the beastly thing is not up to length. However.

I was glad to have the letter. I never have found you ready to misunderstand. But I knew I had been in a hurry & a whirl. So I am glad to know I didn't make a mess.

Moore was excellent in principle. But in condemning Frost I think still that he had been misled into supposing that Frost wanted poetry to be colloquial. All he insists on is what he believes he finds in all poets – absolute fidelity to the postures which the voice assumes in the most expressive intimate speech. So long as these tones & postures are there he has not the least objection to any vocabulary whatever or any inversion or variation from the customary grammatical forms of talk. In fact I think he would agree that if these tones & postures survive in a complicated & learned or subtle vocabulary & structure the result is likely to be better than if they survive in the easiest form, that is in the very words & structures of common speech, though that is not easy or prose would be better than it is & survive more often. I feel sure that no one who knows as much as Moore would dispute this, tho I admit I may not have put it in an intelligible & unquestionable form.

Frost's vocabulary & structure deceive the eye sometimes into thinking it is just statement more or less easily put into easy verse forms. But it is not.

His theory is only an attempt to explain & justify observed facts in Shakespeare for example & in his own earliest efforts.

As to my own method I expect it to change if there is anything more than a doting replica of youthful eagerness in this unexpected ebullition. But although it has a plain look it does so far, I think, represent a culmination as a rule, & does not ask or get much correction on paper.

We shall certainly not all go to America. I should go alone if other things fail, & stay perhaps some time looking about. But I am told I shall have to change my spots if I am to get on there – English people say so – & I do not really know of a method of doing so. I do not know what I shall do before going. I shall have to let you know later whether I can come to you & when. I hope if I can you will be free. But it is not certain I can afford it.

By the way my travelling companion as far as Stroud (Jesse Berridge) and I stopped one night at Ransome's – with *Mrs* Ransome – & had a most pleasant time. I must say I like her very much & can't think why she married such a great man. She still has an irreducible maximum of admiration and affection for him. ... The place is however very full of him, his pipes & books, photographs of him, certificates of prizes which his white mice have won &c. You know it is close to another great home, Beckford's Fonthill.

Yours ever with love to Emily
Edward Thomas

Haymaking

Steep, 6, 7, and 8 July 1915

After night's thunder far away had rolled
The fiery day had a kernel sweet of cold,
And in the perfect blue the clouds uncurled,
Like the first gods before they made the world
And misery, swimming the stormless sea
In beauty and in divine gaiety.
The smooth white empty road was lightly strewn
With leaves – the holly's Autumn falls in June –
And fir cones standing stiff up in the heat.
The mill-foot water tumbled white and lit
With tossing crystals, happier than any crowd
Of children pouring out of school aloud.
And in the little thickets where a sleeper
For ever might lie lost, the nettle-creeper
And garden warbler sang unceasingly;
While over them shrill shrieked in his fierce glee
The swift with wings and tail as sharp and narrow
As if the bow had flown off with the arrow.
Only the scent of woodbine and hay new-mown
Travelled the road. In the field sloping down,
Park-like, to where its willows showed the brook,
Haymakers rested. The tosser lay forsook
Out in the sun; and the long waggon stood
Without its team; it seemed it never would
Move from the shadow of that single yew.
The team, as still, until their task was due,
Beside the labourers enjoyed the shade
That three squat oaks mid-field together made
Upon a circle of grass and weed uncut,
And on the hollow, once a chalk-pit, but
Now brimmed with nut and elder-flower so clean.
The men leaned on their rakes, about to begin,
But still. And all were silent. All was old,
This morning time, with a great age untold,
Older than Clare and Cowper, Morland and Crome,
Than, at the field's far edge, the farmer's home,
A white house crouched at the foot of a great tree.
Under the heavens that know not what years be

The men, the beasts, the trees, the implements
Uttered even what they will in times far hence –
All of us gone out of the reach of change –
Immortal in a picture of an old grange.

Gordon Bottomley, 'Beam-verses at Well Knowe', dated 1899 in *Poems of Thirty Years* (London: Constable, 1925)

Thomas quoted the whole of this poem in his *Daily Chronicle* review of S.F.A. Caulfield's *Home Mottoes and Inscriptions, Old and New* (8 January 1903).

This land was once the Northmen's rest
And here the Virgin's house was blest
With a sweet peace through lost years wrought –
O, in these weary years of nought,
May we who now this hearth-fire light
Learn somewhat of that old delight,
Which, cherished in this drowsy grange,
Shall help the outworn world to change.

A Dream [Sonnet 1]

Steep, 7 and 8 July 1915

Over known fields with an old friend in dream
I walked, but came sudden to a strange stream.
Its dark waters were bursting out most bright
From a great mountain's heart into the light.
They ran a short course under the sun, then back
Into a pit they plunged, once more as black
As at their birth: and I stood thinking there
How white, had the day shone on them, they were,
Heaving and coiling. So by the roar and hiss
And by the mighty motion of the abyss
I was bemused, that I forgot my friend
And neither saw nor sought him till the end,
When I awoke from waters unto men
Saying: 'I shall be here some day again.'

Letter to Robert Frost, 22 July 1915

The words recorded at the end of this letter refer to lines in an
earlier draft of 'A Dream'. This letter also reveals that Thomas
began writing 'A Dream' with the last line, as he did with 'The
long small room'.

13 Rusham Rd, Balham, London SW,
My dear Robert,   22 July 1915

Your letter of July 8 makes rather sore reading for me now, sitting in
the king's uniform in the rain with a bad heel. That is how it began.
Six hours drill & a heavy boot pressing on the big tendon. They say
it is not hopeless. It is not my idea of pleasure, but I do want to go
right through. My idea of pleasure would be getting in 'head first up
to my ankles in (farm) filth & hard work'. But it was too pleasant. I
really couldn't imagine it leading to a living. I would plough & hoe &
reap & sow & be a farmer's boy, but without any certainty & not the
smallest private means I couldn't set out as you did. It isn't in me. Of
course I know I shouldn't starve & that that is all I can say of literary
life here. I could not ask my father for anything. He has no more than
he needs, tho it is true that he & my mother have more or less under-
taken to look after my family if – But try & forgive me everything by

thinking what an asset I shall be in summer camp if I have been in the trenches as well as at Oxford. I believe you know that to find myself living near you & not working for editors would be better than anything I ever did & better than I dare expect. There is no one to keep me here except my mother. She might come too. But I couldn't in this present mess pack up & get born again in New Hampshire I couldn't have before I took the King's shilling. Now of course I have to wait till the war's over.

But it is hopeless *writing* about these things, & I haven't talked about them since you went. I am hampered, too, by knowing that you have hardly heard yet that I thought of enlisting. Perhaps I ought to wait now till I have had a letter back after you heard that & not go on criss-crossing letters so.

A month or two [ago] I dreamt we were walking near Ledington but we lost one another in a strange place & I woke saying to myself 'somehow someday I shall be here again' which I made the last line of some verses.

I want to hear that you really have the farm, & that you like the school better than Elinor thought you would, or rather the children attending it.

We don't know yet whether Scott wants to keep Mervyn till December but if he does he will stay there (or with you) and return in time for Christmas here.

Yours ever
Edward Thomas

Aspens

All day and night, save winter, every weather,
Above the inn, the smithy, and the shop,
The aspens at the cross-roads talk together
Of rain, until their last leaves fall from the top.

Out of the blacksmith's cavern comes the ringing
Of hammer, shoe, and anvil; out of the inn
The clink, the hum, the roar, the random singing –
The sounds that for these fifty years have been.

The whisper of the aspens is not drowned,
And over lightless pane and footless road,
Empty as sky, with every other sound
Not ceasing, calls their ghosts from their abode,

A silent smithy, a silent inn, nor fails
In the bare moonlight or the thick-furred gloom,
In tempest or the night of nightingales,
To turn the cross-roads to a ghostly room.

And it would be the same were no house near.
Over all sorts of weather, men, and times,
Aspens must shake their leaves and men may hear
But need not listen, more than to my rhymes.

Whatever wind blows, while they and I have leaves
We cannot other than an aspen be
That ceaselessly, unreasonably grieves,
Or so men think who like a different tree.

Eleanor Farjeon, 'Poplars at Night', *Dream-Songs for the Beloved* (London: Orpheus Press, The Orpheus Series, 5, Spring, 1911)

Dream-Songs for the Beloved was produced in connection with *Orpheus*, a magazine of mystical art. Thomas contributed prose pieces to *Orpheus* in 1910 and April 1913.

There are no trees so eloquent with wind
As poplars in the moon-mist of the dusk
When like a spirit that has slipt the husk
Among their heavenly crests its breath is thinned.

Their talk is of such high strange mysteries
They must commune in whispers lest weak men
Ere they are ripe for knowledge snatch again
The secret God has given to the trees.

**Robert Frost, 'The Sound of Trees' in *Poetry and Drama*, ed.
Harold Munro (London: Poetry Bookshop, December 1914),
published as 'The Sound of the Trees' in *Mountain Interval*
(New York: Henry Holt, 1916)**

I wonder about the trees.
Why do we wish to bear
Forever the noise of these
More than another noise
So close to our dwelling place?
We suffer them by the day
Till we lose all measure of pace,
And fixity in our joys,
And acquire a listening air.
They are that that talks of going
But never gets away;
And that talks no less for knowing,
As it grows wiser and older,
That now it means to stay.
My feet tug at the floor
And my head sways to my shoulder
Sometimes when I watch the trees sway
From the window or the door.
I shall set forth for somewhere,
I shall make the reckless choice
Some day when they are in voice
And tossing so as to scare
The white clouds over them on.
I shall have less to say,
But I shall be gone.

Edward Thomas's Poets

John Freeman, 'Listening', *Stone Trees* (London: Selwyn and Blount, 1916)

There is a place of grass
With daisies like white pools,
Or shining islands in a sea
Of brightening waves.

Swallows, darting, brush
The waves of gentle green,
As though a wide still lake it were,
Not living grass.

Evening draws over all,
Grass and flowers and sky,
And one rich bird prolongs the sweet
Of day on the edge of dark.

The grass is dim, the stars
Lean down the height of heaven;
And the trees, listening in all their leaves,
Scarce-breathing stand.

Nothing is as it was:
The bird on the bough sings on;
The night, pure from the cloud of day,
Is listening.

Letters to John Freeman and Eleanor Farjeon, 8 June 1915 and 21 July 1915

The letter to Freeman discusses Freeman's 'Listening' and refers to Thomas's belief that in composition conception and execution occur simultaneously. The letter to Eleanor Farjeon gives a clear interpretation of the last lines of 'Aspens'.

My dear Freeman,   Steep, 8 June 1915

I am sorry to be slow but I am thinking & doing nothing but Marlborough. So shall not be up this week. Possibly I may be next if I have the end in sight and I may be able to see you. My evening hours are deeply filled with preparing for the next day's writing. But I have read and re-read your poems as best I could. I liked the trees listening in all their leaves & I felt quite clever to notice by the 5th verse that you weren't rhyming which is as you wished I think. 'In & Out' too I like. But by I know not what perverseness I see in the others – I imagine I see – your intentions as I go along & then refuse to see that you made me see it. That is what I am just discovering is the ghastly result of reviewing. I have concentrated so much on details & side issues that I really am almost impervious to effects. This is how professional critics must have always gone wrong. They like or think they like one method, & not another, & let the principal thing, the effect, go hang, instead of watching first & last for that. Now I see your Goddess plain but imagine it is common property in men of 30 & over & that you just let me into your mind that far but have not done more than remind me that so you & I do feel from time to time. Here I have an idea I am right. The same also applies to 'How should she not forget'. I should say that as it stands it just presents the subject like the Goddess, & is not a thing that exists apart from one's recognising that it is a subject that might be treated. I don't mean that great poems do not remind one of one's own experiences but I believe that they are so complete that one does not see the subject apart from the presentation & could not imagine them done otherwise. On the other hand I plead guilty to being quite capable of missing the *effect* by looking, as I said before, at the process of the treatment, as if it was a thing apart, as if I believed (like Monro) that conception & execution were different things. I admit they may seem so but then it may mean either that the writer is unsuccessful or that the reader is not understanding, is cautious, or a professional critic like

Yours ever
Edward Thomas
I will let you know if I come up and have free time.

My dear Eleanor   13 Rusham Rd, Balham, Tuesday,
                                           postmarked 21 July 1915

I got your letter and the typescript on Sunday night but we had a visitor till Sunday afternoon and I was very full up. Then yesterday I was attested and today I did six hours drill. There is a great deal to tell you yet I can't promise to see you yet. My feet have already given me the trouble I long ago foresaw. It may be curable. I am to see the doctor about it tomorrow. But it puts me in a rather miserable position if it can't be mended. However, don't you worry. It's only silly to be in uniform and useless, but I shall get over it one way or the other.

About 'Aspens' you missed just the turn that I thought essential. *I* was the aspen. 'We' meant the trees and I with my dejected shyness. Does that clear it up, or do you think in rereading it that I have not emphasised it enough?

Don't think this only another of my excuses for not writing a letter, though it is an excuse for not writing now the one I could have written on Sunday if I had not been so occupied. I only send it because I have waited long already. Otherwise I should wait longer till I had seen the doctor. I only hope he won't give me the leisure to think why I joined. Several people *have* asked me, but I could not answer yet.

You had a beautiful Sunday, I should think; we did, so warm, clear and fresh. But I am not writing weather rhymes again yet.

Yours ever

Edward Thomas

Digging [2]
('What matter makes my spade for tears or mirth')
London, 21 July 1915

What matter makes my spade for tears or mirth,
Letting down two clay pipes into the earth?
The one I smoked, the other a soldier
Of Blenheim, Ramillies, and Malplaquet
Perhaps. The dead man's immortality
Lies represented lightly with my own,
A yard or two nearer the living air
Than bones of ancients who, amazed to see
Almighty God erect the mastodon,
Once laughed, or wept, in this same light of day.

Letters to Eleanor Farjeon, 21 and 26 July 1915

These letters record a frequent topic of discussion between
Thomas and Farjeon – that of rhyme. In the second letter he
also makes a connection between poetry composition and the
weather ('rainy afternoon').

My dear Eleanor,   13 Rusham Rd, 21 July 1915

I have just got to wait and see. The army doctor is giving me some
treatment and some rest. But I can't manage anything this week
because I have 2 books to do in my spare time. I was a bad prophet,
because I have been perspiring these six hours over ten lines which
perhaps are not right yet. But if you would type them for me I could
see them better. They are

What matter makes my spade for tears or mirth,
Letting down two old pipes into the earth?
The one I smoked, the other a soldier
Of Blenheim, Ramillies, and Malplaquet
Perhaps. The dead man's immortality
Lies lightly represented with my own,
A yard or two nearer the air of day
Than bones of ancients who, amazed to see
Almighty God erect the mastodon
Once laughed or wept at what earth had to bear.

I suppose it should have been a sonnet, but I can't Rawnsleyise yet.

I believe you were right to be uncertain about Miss ——. I am so glad I wasn't there, though I should like to have seen you and Arnold and Daphne and Undine. Helen and I had a lovely walk. She will be glad to have you over from Singleton. I only hope I shall not be there. I do want to go on now. I don't want to see anybody till I know if I can. God bless you.

Yours ever

Edward Thomas

Don't tell anybody I aren't a soldier yet tho I am in uniform.

My dear Eleanor   13 Rusham Rd, Balham SW,
                                          postmarked 26 July 1915

The exams rather exploded the verses, but I have a laugh at you for not detecting the rhyme of soldier and bear. However to please you I bring the rhyme nearer. I send you also 2 other rainy afternoon efforts. In case you are free tomorrow (Tuesday) at x I will come to lunch then at the Lyons nearest the top of Tottenham Court Rd on the left going N. I will come through to the back. But I may have a very bare hour. Don't trouble to write even if you can't come. I will be there unless the sergeant says no.

Yours ever

Edward Thomas

Cock-Crow

London, 23 July 1915

Out of the wood of thoughts that grows by night
To be cut down by the sharp axe of light, –
Out of the night, two cocks together crow,
Cleaving the darkness with a silver blow:
And bright before my eyes twin trumpeters stand,
Heralds of splendour, one at either hand,
Each facing each as in a coat of arms:
The milkers lace their boots up at the farms.

Gordon Bottomley, 'Song VIII: Elegiac Mood', 'Night and Morning Songs' (1896–1909), *Chambers of Imagery* II (London: Elkin Mathews, 1912)

Bottomley's 'Song VIII', shares with 'Cock-Crow' its concluding movement from the heraldic or heroic to the mundane.

From song and dream for ever gone
Are Helen, Helen of Troy,
And Cleopatra made to look upon,
And many a daring boy –
Young Faust and Sigurd and Hippolytus:
They are twice dead and we must find
Great ladies yet unblemished by the mind,
Heroes and acts not cold for us
In amber or spirits of too many words.
Ay, these are murdered by much thinking on.
I hanker even for new shapes of swords,
More different sins, and raptures not yet done.
Yet, as I wait on marvels, such a bird
As maybe Sigurd heard –
A thrush – alighting with a little run
Out-tops the daisies as it passes
And peeps bright-eyed above the grasses.

Letter to Gordon Bottomley, 26 May 1912

Thomas admires Bottomley's 'Elegiac Mood' for its change in diction, from a heroic recounting of the deeds of legendary

Edward Thomas's Poets

figures that makes heavy use of abstract nouns such as 'acts', 'spirits', 'shapes', 'sins', 'raptures' and 'marvels', to the plain simple details of the movements of one bird. Thomas uses a similar shift in his 'Cock-Crow', dropping in tone as he moves from the heraldic image of cocks as two trumpeters or 'heralds of splendour' 'cleaving the darkness' to a simple description of milkers lacing up their boots.

Dillybrook Farm, Road, nr Bath,

My dear Gordon,   26 May 1912 (Here till about June 10)

I am writing the first and worst book on Swinburne & very busy but have not forgotten the mean letter I wrote to you before I discovered what fine things you put into Babel for example & what a sweet thing that Thrush was that destroyed your Diction so. But writing books on Hearn Pater & Swinburne has ruined me for anything but fault-finding. So far I have done nothing else with Swinburne, only I still find 'In an Orchard' & 'Itylus' & the 'Ballad of Life' lovely. Here the train begins to move so I will only say I send de la Mare's book to show I love you & hope this May has done you good. Tell us.

Yours Ever
Edward Thomas

Letter to W.H. Hudson, 20 November 1914

The lines quoted in this letter come from Thomas Hardy's war poem, 'Men Who March Away', dated 5 September 1914 and published in the *Times* on 9 September 1914 as 'Song of the Soldiers'. Thomas used an extract from it as an epigraph in *This England*. Hardy's exploration of the image of crowing barn-cocks resembles Thomas's similar image in 'Cock-Crow'.

My dear Hudson,   Steep, Petersfield, 20 November 1914

It seems a great age since I saw you at St Luke's Rd. Garnett told me long after that you were still not well, but had got as far away as Ascot. My excuse for writing now is to ask for news both of yourself and of Garnett. All I can hear of him is that he went to France 'for an indefinite period' a fortnight ago. So they told me at Duckworth's. I have no news of myself. As you will have supposed I have not enlisted, tho I should have done had I been in company that had encouraged me. At least I think so. Not that I pretend to be warlike or to think except with blank misgiving of any sort of life different from my past: only I can't justify not making an effort, except by saying that if I did go it would be hard to put and leave things straight at home. It is just a little too late to jump at so very complete a release from the mess of journalism. The only pleasure I have had in that lately has been reading the best of Wilfrid Blunt's *Poems*. I wonder have you known them all long ago? 'Esther' was new to me. So was 'Worth Forest'. It is curious how he is always either absolutely good and true, or quite euphemistic, periphrastic and worthless. But with it all, I would as soon lose almost any of the Victorians except Arnold and perhaps Tennyson and the better Meredith. Nobody has sent me Hardy's latest. I thought his poem in the *Times*

Ere the barn cocks say
Night is growing grey,

the only good one connected with the war.

We were all in Gloucestershire, near Ledbury, for August. I saw something of Abercrombie. We went to Tewkesbury together. But I was mostly with Frost on short excursions, seldom further than Whiteleaved Oak, at our end of the Malverns. Did you ever see it or hear of its alleged little dark inhabitants with gruff monosyllabic names? I could not find them. Now Abercrombie who has lost practically all his work has gone away with his family to a house belonging to Hewlett's sister in Lincolnshire. Frost is staying on in England for a time. Rupert Brooke was in the trenches at Antwerp, which is the most I have heard of a poet so far. There are so many one could have sacrificed, too.

I hope Mrs Hudson has gone on improving.

Yours ever

Edward Thomas

October
High Beech, Essex, 15–16 October 1915

The green elm with the one great bough of gold
Lets leaves into the grass slip, one by one. –
The short hill grass, the mushrooms small milk-white,
Harebell and scabious and tormentil,
That blackberry and gorse, in dew and sun,
Bow down to; and the wind travels too light
To shake the fallen birch leaves from the fern;
The gossamers wander at their own will.
At heavier steps than birds' the squirrels scold.

The late year has grown fresh again and new
As Spring, and to the touch is not more cool
Than it is warm to the gaze; and now I might
As happy be as earth is beautiful,
Were I some other or with earth could turn
In alternation of violet and rose,
Harebell and snowdrop, at their season due,
And gorse that has no time not to be gay.
But if this be not happiness, who knows?
Some day I shall think this a happy day,
And this mood by the name of melancholy
Shall no more blackened and obscured be.

Letters to Eleanor Farjeon, October 1915

The close connection for Thomas between letter-writing and
poetry composition is indicated when he offers Farjeon
'October' as a letter. He also implies a close connection between
periods of physical disability – such as an injured knee – and his
acts of poetic composition. He discusses the rhyme, accent and
flowers in 'October' and refers to a previous draft.

My dear Eleanor   High Beech, 17 October 1915

Will you take some verses for a letter? I have been lame with an
injured knee 2 days and this is what I have done with them and can't
write a letter as good as yours that I got this morning. There's little
to tell you anyhow. It has been a bad week with full evenings. If my

knee is no better tomorrow I have some hope of getting leave to go off home for 2 or 3 days. But we may be starting musketry tomorrow and in that case I should have to try to do it, as it is the one thing they do well here. The rumours about a change of camp are not anything more yet. Most people hope to go to London and I should if we had done our musketry, as there would then be little to learn here that could not be as well learnt at headquarters.

How I envy you getting here and there in this fine weather as I used to do. If I am in town for a few hours I will try to arrange to see you.

Have you time to make some copies of these 21 lines?

Tchaikovsky it was I expect.

Goodbye.

Yours ever

Edward Thomas

My dear Eleanor   Here [London], Sunday [October 1915]

We have just missed here. I didn't keep you waiting yesterday I hope. We were not dismissed till 5. And now I am leaving to go back to High Beech. Helen will tell you the change. I am only sorry because it means not being in town. It will be fully a fortnight before I get up again.

Are you quite well again? Typing for me somehow corresponds to your diseases, but I hope doesn't produce them. I expect you're right about the rhymes, most of them. The original version was in blank verse, but quite different. Hasn't Bronwen taught you tormentil, the tiny yellow flower in short hill grass, a flat buttercup or avens with rather separate petals? Tormentilla it is. The accent is on the 2nd syllable which doesn't (as I see it) affect the merit of the line whatever it may be; I mean doesn't tell against it. I suppose the influence of High Beech and the Artists ought to be clearer. I am going to slightly better conditions, but don't expect to write till I am disabled again. The knee is now well. My new address will be

A Company
  Artists Rifles
    Suntrap
      High Beech
I go on Tuesday afternoon.

I believe I have floundered over refusing a wristwatch from Bertie and Joan. But I really didn't want one.

Yours ever

Edward Thomas

Letter to John Freeman, 26 October 1915

My dear Freeman,   13 Rusham Rd, 26 October 1915

I was very sorry indeed not to see you and to know you were prob-
ably waiting there. But I have been wretchedly driven and am now in
a bit of a mess. Yesterday I thought I was off to High Beech on
Tuesday to join A Company and study maps in particular. Now I
have been held up in the transfer and don't know where I shall be. If
it means a delay of a week in town I shan't mind and will let you know.
I have rewritten those lines. Did you mean the one that now runs

> And gorse that has no time to be gay?

But I am most disinclined to write now in this uncertainty, and have
to pack in case I do go. Added to which I have acquired a nasty disease
of the skin of the face – barber's rash. In fact I don't like things at all.
But never mind. I hope I shall see you soon.

    Yours ever

        Edward Thomas

There's nothing like the sun
Hare Hall Camp, 18–19 November 1915

There's nothing like the sun as the year dies,
Kind as it can be, this world being made so,
To stones and men and beasts and birds and flies,
To all things that it touches except snow,
Whether on mountain side or street of town.
The south wall warms me: November has begun,
Yet never shone the sun as fair as now
While the sweet last-left damsons from the bough
With spangles of the morning's storm drop down
Because the starling shakes it, whistling what
Once swallows sang. But I have not forgot
That there is nothing, too, like March's sun,
Like April's, or July's, or June's, or May's,
Or January's, or February's, great days:
And August, September, October, and December
Have equal days, all different from November.
No day of any month but I have said –
Or, if I could live long enough, should say –
'There's nothing like the sun that shines today.'
There's nothing like the sun till we are dead.

Letters to Eleanor Farjeon, November and December 1915

These letters reveal the physical conditions in which 'There's nothing like the sun' was written, and detail of its successive revisions. In the second letter Thomas connects proverbs and local sayings in his *Four-and-Twenty Blackbirds* with his work as a poet.

Wednesday, Hut 23, Harehall Camp,
My dear Eleanor   Gidea Park, Romford, Essex

I should have written before but I did not know where I should be. And I don't know now, but they say it will be here for some time, though our officer has gone back to London and expected we should soon follow him. We are having too easy a time, so that again I have reverted and written some verses. I am afraid they aren't finished. I never have any time really to myself and have continually to be putting my paper away. The days we spend in more or less formally examining the country with a view to taking classes out though we do not know that we shall have to do so. Beautiful cold sunny days, and the earth thick with clean snow. I will copy out the verses as they exist now and if you like them will you make a copy or two of them?

There's nothing like the sun as the year dies,
Kind as it can be, this world being so,
To stones and men and beasts and trees and flies,
To all things that it touches except snow,
Whether on mountain side or street of town.
The south wall warms me. November has begun
Yet never shone the sun as fair as now
While the sweet last-left damsons from the bough
With spangles of the morning's storm drop down
Because the starling shakes it, whistling what
Once swallows sang. Yet I can forget not
That there is nothing, too, like March's sun,
Like April's, or July's or June's or May's,
Or January's or February's great days;
August, September, October and December
Have equal days, all different from November.
No day of any month but I have said —
Or if I could live long enough should say —
There's nothing like the sun shining today —
There's nothing like the sun till a man's dead.

The camp is excellent but on the dullest flattest piece of a beautiful piece of country. I have a new set of people to get used to but have too transitory a feeling to succeed rapidly. Now a man has come along to talk and I must shut this up for tomorrow morning's post. The end of last week got full up and I went home again on Friday till Sunday morning.
        Yours ever
        Edward Thomas

My dear Eleanor   Train to Petersfield,
                              postmarked 28 November 1915

Thank you again. Now I am going home and I will type the thing yet again because I have touched it again. I had great trouble to get leave this week end, but here I am in a train which ought ultimately to reach

Petersfield. I tried to think how I could see you in town, but there is only Sunday and I have got to see my Mother and there is only Sunday afternoon possible and London then is not kind. The leave I half expected in the middle of the week didn't come off. I just got up to see the dentist, but without warning enough to let you know. With that interval this week has been much like the last, with some beautiful but cold weather that doesn't cure colds when you stand about drawing. Still we had always a solid hour for lunch in a farm or pub and got to know one another a bit. Next week may bring a change, a real job, and a move to a new company without a terrier for a sergeant major – but not in town it seems. With luck I may be home for Christmas but not to meet Mervyn. I only hope the mail won't cheat him of his fare.

By the time I am a sergeant I shall be really young I suppose. I wish I had gone on where the Proverbs left off. Probably I never shall, unless 'Lob' is the beginning.

Goodbye. I will finish this at Steep or at any rate add a copy of the lines.

Ever yours
Edward Thomas

My dear Eleanor   Hut 35 [undated]

Thank you very much. You will see I have made just 2 or 3 slight changes. 'This world being made so' is 5 heavy syllables unaccented. I hope you won't object but if you do I want to know. Thus far I had written when I began to be interrupted, and now it is near closing time. Tomorrow I am to see the doctor. I have been rather bad for 3 days and may get some days' leave and see you in the course of them; which must atone (if it can) for this short letter. We are now supposed to be fixed here though we still have to find our own work for the day. Some of the men are very interesting and altogether days pass easily – a little too easily. I prefer it to a lot of Gunn though. I know what you feel about Cliffords, in fact I think I feel as you do. Yours by the way, is the only reference I have seen yet to 4 and 20 Blackbirds. No reviews. No anything. But I am not complaining except of my cold &c which almost makes me write again – not quite, because it is too lowering. Who is the Scavenger Poet? Is he the last desperate effort of the people who discovered Davies had a wooden leg and wished he had 2? Helen sounds well again. But Frost is silent now.

Goodbye
Edward Thomas

My dear Eleanor   A Company now, postmarked 3 December 1915

I wonder if you are right. In any case you have set me turning the thing over again and you will see the result in this copy. If you can bring yourself to, will you make a copy or two? The last line brings us two back again. But there is not much time now because we have really begun to work. We have a five days course, five days on end with a platoon of 50 men beginning (as far as possible) at the point where they left off at October in town. We don't have a Saturday class – all are out of doors – and I have now got into a new company with a sweeter sergeant-major so that I may get this week end and go to Coventry and see Hodson about Mervyn. Mervyn's last letter was largely about ships he might come by, and we shall soon look for news of the day of sailing. But I shan't be able to meet him. If I go to Coventry and have any time in London on my way I will try to arrange (if you are free) to see you. Goodbye.
  Yours ever
  Edward Thomas

The Thrush

Hare Hall Camp, November 1915
'the day I was in as hut-orderly while the rest went to South Weald'

When Winter's ahead,
What can you read in November
That you read in April
When Winter's dead?

I hear the thrush, and I see
Him alone at the end of the lane
Near the bare poplar's tip,
Singing continuously.

Is it more that you know
Than that, even as in April,
So in November,
Winter is gone that must go?

Or is all your lore
Not to call November November,
And April April,
And Winter Winter – no more?

But I know the months all,
And their sweet names, April,
May and June and October,
As you call and call

I must remember
What died into April
And consider what will be born
Of a fair November;

And April I love for what
It was born of, and November
For what it will die in,
What they are and what they are not,

While you love what is kind,
What you can sing in

And love and forget in
All that's ahead and behind.

**Gordon Bottomley, 'Eager Spring', *Chambers of Imagery* II
(London: Elkin Mathews, 1912)**

Like 'The Thrush', this poem addresses a loved one, although
more gently. It, too, focuses on the song of a thrush, while
declaring the presence of the coming spring in winter. Thomas
anthologised 'Eager Spring' in *This England* (1915), and in
Flowers I Love (1916).

Whirl, snow, on the blackbird's chatter;
You will not hinder his song to come.
East wind, Sleepless, you cannot scatter
Quince-bud, almond-bud,
Little grape-hyacinth's
Clustering brood,
Nor unfurl the tips of the plum.
No half-born stalk of a lily stops;
There is sap in the storm-torn bush;
And, ruffled by gusts in a snow-blurred copse,
'Pity to wait' sings a thrush.

Love, there are few Springs left for us;
They go, and the count of them as they go
Makes surer the count that is left for us.
More than the East wind, more than the snow,
I would put back these hours that bring
Buds and bees and are lost;
I would hold the night and the frost,
To save for us one more Spring.

This is no case of petty right or wrong
Steep, 26 December 1915

This is no case of petty right or wrong
That politicians or philosophers
Can judge. I hate not Germans, nor grow hot
With love of Englishmen, to please newspapers.
Beside my hate for one fat patriot
My hatred of the Kaiser is love true: –
A kind of god he is, banging a gong.
But I have not to choose between the two,
Or between justice and injustice. Dinned
With war and argument I read no more
Than in the storm smoking along the wind
Athwart the wood. Two witches' cauldrons roar.
From one the weather shall rise clear and gay;
Out of the other an England beautiful
And like her mother that died yesterday.
Little I know or care if, being dull,
I shall miss something that historians
Can rake out of the ashes when perchance
The phoenix broods serene above their ken.
But with the best and meanest Englishmen
I am one in crying, God save England, lest
We lose what never slaves and cattle blessed.
The ages made her that made us from the dust:
She is all we know and live by, and we trust
She is good and must endure, loving her so:
And as we love ourselves we hate her foe.

Letters to Robert Frost and Eleanor Farjeon, 9 August 1915 and 7 January 1916

The accounts of Thomas's arguments with his father suggest the genesis of 'This is no petty case of right or wrong'. The 'couplets' at the end of the Farjeon letter refer to 'The Thrush'.

	(but Steep will	13 Rusham Rd,
My dear Robert	always (D.v.) find me)	9 August 1915

I am a real soldier now, inoculated and all. My foot has come round

& I am rather expecting to go right through my 3 or 4 months training
& already wondering what regiment I shall get a commission in. It
seems I am too old to get a commission for immediate foreign service.
That is, at present. They are raising the age by degrees. As things are
now I should spend at any rate some months with my regiment in
England, perhaps even find myself in one only for home service. But
I want to see what it is like out there. It has made a change. I have had
3 weeks of free evenings & haven't been able to get my one surviving
review written. The training makes the body insist on real leisure. All
I am left fit for is talk & cleaning my brass buttons & badge. Not much
talk – either here or at the headquarters. The men are too young or
the wrong kind, mostly. But I see Ellis, Davies & de la Mare &
Freeman now & then. Also I have had 24 hours at home twice. I drill,
clean rifles, wash out lavatories &c. Soon I shall be standing sentry in
the street in my turn. In a fortnight I hope to be in camp at Epping
Forest. I stand very nearly as straight as a lamp post & apparently get
smaller every week in the waist & have to get new holes punched in
my belt. The only time now I can think of verses is on sleepless nights,
but I don't write them down. Say Thank you.

They are very well at home. Helen has Mrs Ellis with her for a time.
Bronwen has holidays now & expects to be invited away. The cottage
is to be let for September & the family to scatter a bit. Ledington &
White leaved Oak seems purely paradisial, with Beauty of Bath apples
Hesperidean lying with thunder dew on the warm ground. I am
almost old enough not to make any moan of it.

You are not going to tell me I ought to have had the courage *not*
to do this. Jack Collings Squire argues it requires more courage *not*
to. It is strange how few people one knows at it. Edward Garnett has
gone out with an ambulance corps to the Italian front. Masefield is
doing something in connection with a hospital – the papers said he
was working as an orderly – I heard he was organizing. Hulme (I
understand) is actually out in or near the fighting line. 'Blast' has
executed a second number. Harrison continues to exhort and the
'Times' reissues the poems we didn't admit in August with illustra-
tions. Do you hear of Chandler?

People get fined occasionally for speaking well of the Germans at
private parties – under the Defence of the Realm Act. I don't wonder.
My father is so rampant in his cheery patriotism that I become pro-
German every evening. We can never so beat the Germans that they
will cease to remember their victories. Pom-pom. I am sorry. The
post interrupted this with a letter from Miss Farjeon who is distrib-
uting herself about the country – as usual. Nothing from you yet. I

will keep this back till tomorrow in case. – But today has been too full & as I have a long march tomorrow I won't get up to remedy this but just send my love to you all.

Yours ever
Edward Thomas

D Company, Hut 51, postmarked Ilford

My dear Eleanor   7 January 1916

Thank you very much. I am not sure that 'love true' is a mistake, but perhaps 'love I will not' is, and I suggest

... Philosophers
Can see] I hate not Germans, nor grow hot
with love of English, to please newspapers.

But perhaps it won't do. I am so busy now. The move to this new hut and company means a lot of new responsibility. Being senior corporal in the hut I am in charge of it, have to appoint men to clean it etc, call the roll and stop talking after lights out etc. Very possibly there will be more to do soon. Nor shall we have every week-end. Also every morning we waste over an hour in mere parade drill with our company. We can't get up just for the day on Saturday or Sunday as we could before. I am not enjoying it really. I have been out of sorts since last Saturday when I came up to town and saw my father and got into a very unpleasant argument. However I have some hope of getting home tomorrow night or Sunday.

I did write the couplets at Steep, but the others some weeks ago here. Helen won't like them a bit and I kept them by me undecided. I hope you are right.

Probably I shan't go to Coventry with Mervyn. When I shall get any time in town next, who knows?

Yours ever
Edward Thomas

1916

Song [2] ('The clouds that are so light')

Hare Hall, 15 January 1916

The clouds that are so light,
Beautiful, swift and bright,
Cast shadows on field and park
Of the earth that is so dark,

And even so now, light one!
Beautiful, swift and bright one!
You let fall on a heart that was dark,
Unillumined, a deeper mark.

But clouds would have, without earth
To shadow, far less worth:
Away from your shadow on me
Your beauty less would be,

And if it still be treasured
An age hence, it shall be measured
By this small dark spot
Without which it were not.

Letter to Eleanor Farjeon, 15 January 1916

The first paragraph of this letter shows a connection between
Thomas's experience of working outdoors, boredom, lack of
activity and the writing of the 'conceit', 'The clouds that are so
light'.

My dear Eleanor   Hut 15 now! Saturday [15 January 1916]

I have got 2 hours to myself in the hut, having set free the man who was supposed to look after it till all came in. Half are away on weekend leave & all that I care for. All day I have had nothing to do & no freedom to go more than 2 miles out. I did 2 panoramas for practice, but it was a beautiful day thrown away. These 2 hours I didn't really know what to do with. This conceit is the result: –

[The text of 'The clouds that are so light']

Is it worth typing? I sent you 2 others last Sunday on my way home. It was the *Thrush* that Helen didn't like.

I got into trouble soon after my return. Mason was away till the same Sunday night and was not in at roll-call, but feeling sure he would be in by the next train, I reported him present. He didn't return till 7 a.m. on Monday, by which time I had reported him absent in a fluster. So we both had 2 serious talks with the Sergeant Major & an Officer, & my position isn't improved. I shan't be a full corporal just yet.

So you have a white blackbird. Good luck to you and it. It is certain to be a white blackbird. It will have a better chance in Hampstead than ours had at Steep. We saw it for 3 years though.

Things aren't at their best. The new responsibilities & the trouble upset me. Then Christmas perhaps. And the new rule against going more than 2 miles out of camp makes Saturday & Sunday days of imprisonment. I only hope I shall get off next week.

Goodbye. Yours ever
Edward Thomas

Roads

'Coming home from Hare Hall', 22 January 1916

I love roads:
The goddesses that dwell
Far along invisible
Are my favourite gods.

Roads go on
While we forget, and are
Forgotten like a star
That shoots and is gone.

On this earth 'tis sure
We men have not made
Anything that doth fade
So soon, so long endure:

The hill road wet with rain
In the sun would not gleam
Like a winding stream
If we trod it not again.

They are lonely
While we sleep, lonelier
For lack of the traveller
Who is now a dream only.

From dawn's twilight
And all the clouds like sheep
On the mountains of sleep
They wind into the night.

The next turn may reveal
Heaven: upon the crest
The close pine clump, at rest
And black, may Hell conceal.

Often footsore, never
Yet of the road I weary,
Though long and steep and dreary
As it winds on for ever.

1916

Helen of the roads,
The mountain ways of Wales
And the Mabinogion tales,
Is one of the true gods,

Abiding in the trees,
The threes and fours so wise,
The larger companies,
That by the roadside be,

And beneath the rafter
Else uninhabited
Excepting by the dead;
And it is her laughter

At morn and night I hear
When the thrush cock sings
Bright irrelevant things,
And when the chanticleer

Calls back to their own night
Troops that make loneliness
With their light footsteps' press,
As Helen's own are light.

Now all roads lead to France
And heavy is the tread
Of the living; but the dead
Returning lightly dance:

Whatever the road bring
To me or take from me,
They keep me company
With their pattering,

Crowding the solitude
Of the loops over the downs,
Hushing the roar of towns
And their brief multitude.

W.H. Hudson, 'The London Sparrow' (last verse), *Merry England*, 1883–5, in *Dead Man's Plack, An Old Thorn and Poems* (London: Dent, 1924)

The last lines of this long poem act as an echo of the dead's pattering feet in 'Roads'.

> Vanished is my dream;
> Even while I bowed and veiled my eyes before
> The insufferable splendour of the sun
> It vanished quite, and left me with this pale,
> This phantom morning! With my dreams thou fled'st,
> O blithe remembrancer, and in thy flight
> Callest thy prattling fellows, prompters too
> Of dreams perchance, from many a cloudy roof
> To flit, a noisy rain of sparrows, down
> To snatch a hasty breakfast from the roads,
> Undaunted by the thund'rous noise and motion:
> But like the petrel – fearless, fitful seeker,
> The fluctuating bird with ocean's wastes
> And rage familiar, tossed with tossing billows –
> So, gleaner unregarded, flittest thou –
> Now, as of old, and in the years to come,
> Nature's one witness, till the murmuring sound
> Of human feet unnumbered, like the rain
> Of summer pattering on the forest leaves,
> Fainter and fainter falling 'midst the ruin,
> In everlasting silence dies away.

Walter de la Mare, 'Autumn', *Poems* (London: John Murray, 1906)

The first verse of this poem resonates with the sixth verse of 'Roads'. In his 9 November 1906 *Daily Chronicle* review of de la Mare's *Poems* Thomas refers to de la Mare's 'sincerity, speaking, as sincerity always does, a strange new tongue, because it is unlike our muddy conventional speech'. De la Mare repays the compliment, quoting several verses from 'Roads' in his *Times Literary Supplement* review of Thomas's *Last Poems* (2 January 1919).

There is a wind where the rose was;
Cold rain where sweet grass was;
   And clouds like sheep
   Stream o'er the steep
Grey skies where the lark was.

Nought gold where your hair was;
Nought warm where your hand was;
   But phantom, forlorn,
   Beneath the thorn,
Your ghost where your face was.

Sad winds where your voice was;
Tears, tears where my heart was;
   And ever with me,
   Child, ever with me,
Silence where hope was.

John Freeman, 'The Enemies', *Stone Trees* (London: Selwyn and Blount, 1916)

The second verse of this poem, which Thomas critiques in the letter following, resonates with the sixth verse of 'Roads'.

The angry wind
That cursed at me
Was nothing but an evil sprite
Vexed with any man's delight.

And strange it seemed
That a dark wind
Should run down from a mountain steep
And shout as though the world were asleep

But when he ceased
And silence was –
Who could but fear what evil sprite
Crept through the tunnels of the night?

Letter to John Freeman, 23 March 1915

John Freeman has pencilled in the comment 'My poor poems!' on this letter. Thomas offers candid criticism of 'The Enemies' and other poems. Some of the poems can be found in *Stone Trees* (1916) and *Memories of Childhood and other poems* (1918). Thomas emphasises his sense of the importance of plain and exact meanings, and questions abstractions.

My dear Freeman,   Steep, Petersfield, [23] March 1915

I like 'The Enemies' even better than I did when you sent it. It seems to be perfect though I prefer the 2nd & 3rd verses: or rather find myself in memory compressing the 1st & 2nd. I think I like 'The noisy fire' as well, though 3 abstract nouns are a lot for 3 verses. The first, by the way, – 'loneliness' – is it quite necessary & is it even quite exact? Do you mean in solitude, or something only 'loneliness' itself does express? Perhaps I ought not to intrude on those inexplicable preferences. I notice the abstract nouns in 'The Death of Kings'. There I feel more that they are part of the abstractness that I can't enjoy & I think that atmosphere has permitted certain too abstract phrases which wouldn't be abstract if they were alive: like 'bitterness of defeat' & 'miracle of youth'. I should always suspect 'miracle of youth' wherever I met it as meaning practically nothing except that the writer wished to show that he felt admiringly towards 'youth'. But perhaps I oughtn't to say. It is in 'The dead light in the field's dead white' again. If only you could have left the reader to intellectualise the scene, the light and the rain would have been lovely. But don't mind me, for I am obviously to some extent colour blind where some of your strongest characteristics are concerned, so that when I read

> That high
> Indifference of starry dust

I just know it must be John Freeman's.

I am being a beast. Now I say why 'guilty trees' of Guinevere & only Guinevere? To use that horrid word that I got on the train last weekend I don't think Guinevere is available. Perhaps she is, but I don't expect ever to be moved by her name anywhere after Morris.

Am I going to make this worse by saying it is part of my growing imperviousness to anything not as plain as pen & ink & bread & butter? You get up again & again – you are up in 'Music Comes' –

where I can't follow. I have to drop like a clog. Most likely you are quite right, & I simply represent the other half of the world, or quarter, or whatever it is. If I knew this was so, I would not mention it. I do so in case it does indicate that you can sometimes be content with what seems the spirit of a thing when you might get at the spirit itself. But I believe rather that it is simply that I live in another land (both England); for even 'Misadventure', 'Fear' & 'Waking' have a quality in common with the others which I am not master of. A line like 'But were as bright as primroses in a dark lane' proves it: so does a sentence like 'Yet a man dying would not with such fear scream out at hell'. In a stranger, I should probably have blundered into the opinion that it was an exaggeration, that perhaps the writer had not heard a dying man scream, whether at hell or not. This is distinctly nasty, isn't it? 'Waking' & 'Away, away' I like best of that set. In fact I like 'Waking' after 'The Enemies' & 'The noisy fire', but less than them because 'a hundred seas of sleep' is not as powerful as it is big.

Now what have I done? Do come down & let us know that we have some Englishness in common. You shan't label me Welsh whatever you do to escape my remarks.

Yours ever
Edward Thomas

Letter to Eleanor Farjeon, 24 January 1916

This letter gives detail, in its second paragraph, of stages in the composition process of 'Roads', suggesting the importance of an element of temporal dislocation in this process. The letter also elaborates on references in the poem, as well as mentioning Thomas's 'Rain'.

My dear Eleanor   Hut 15, 24 January 1916

I have let a long time go by. In the interval I have been home for 24 hours. That is all I could get, and I was really glad to get it, though not so glad by the time I was at Gidea Park again near midnight 5 hours after being home. We all had a long walk in the morning, did odd jobs in the afternoon, went to the Bones for an hour and then parted in a very black night – However my trouble is mostly over, and will be entirely if they allow me to have my 2nd Stripe this week as I should have done.

On the way home I got on with some verses I began last week or at last began thinking towards, and I have now nearly finished them.

I shall try to copy them out for you before I shut this up tonight.

There is not much that is new except these lines about roads.

Certainly I think your dashes would clear up 'Rain' a little. I will put them in.

I would have written yesterday in the train but thought there might be a letter from you waiting in camp and I mustn't write too many. I spend rather more than all my pay now. This is not a very intelligent remark. It simply means that feeling I ought to economise I hit upon the idea of two letters instead of three – And now I expect I shall have a letter as soon as I post this. I hope so.

So you saw Mother. You know I think she was more than pretty, don't you?

They asked for 500 volunteers for a draft to France today. 2 or 3 hours to decide. They might probably not have taken me. Anyway I didn't decide.

16 verses I see it makes. Helen is the lady in the Mabinogion, the Welsh lady who married Maxen the Emperor and gave her name to the great old mountain roads – Sarn Helen they are all marked on the maps. Do you remember the 'Dream of Maxen'? She is known to mythologists as one of the travelling goddesses of the dusk. But perhaps I don't convey much in my 16 verses.

Goodbye. Yours ever
Edward Thomas

Letter to Gordon Bottomley 18 February 1916

This letter discusses Thomas's use of ghosts in 'Roads'.

My dear Gordon,   Hut 15, Hare Hall Camp, 18 February 1916

Thank you for your quick reply. I wish you had liked 'Roads' more. I thought the particular ghosts came in comfortably enough after the ghosts in general. For myself I didn't know whether it came off as a whole or not. – I hope I can find enough suitable things for the anthology. It is very hospitable of Abercrombie & Trevelyan to ask me in, & when I go home in a fortnight's time I will send you a big dose. Will you tell me meantime whether you would rather not have the 2 poems appearing in *Form*? They are 2 you liked most, 'Lob' & 'Words'. If I can find your letter I will see which the poems were that you liked. As a matter of fact one at least occurs in a half dozen that Guthrie is using. 20 pages will give me a chance.

I don't know what exact arrangement you will make with

Constable, but I should say that royalties ought to begin to come in after the sales have reached a certain fixed figure, not after expenses have been paid, which leaves the publisher too free to decide when he begins to pay out. It is extremely rum that Waugh & Tynan should administer the laurels to Mrs Lear, unless it is that they respect the amount of water that has run under London Bridge since you began to publish. I think I heard too that Courtney decided not to admit he wasn't convinced. He is afraid of not going to Heaven with you (or anybody else who may be going).

About the matinée, Romford is only 12 miles from Liverpool St, but the difficulty is I can never get away except on a Saturday morning, so that I couldn't see the play unless it was on a Saturday.

I got back here on Wednesday half-mended, & have had a fairly easy time to get quite well in. Tomorrow I hope I may go to Coventry & see Mervyn at his new last school there.

I had 4 days convalescence at home which I enjoyed, except that I wasn't fit for much except strolling in the sun & sitting down for half an hour to do a panorama. This is one of the gentlest of military arts. I do one or two every week for practice. I can imagine becoming almost good enough to illustrate a travel book or any writing I don't entirely like.

By the way I prefer to remain Eastaway for the time being. People are too likely to be prejudiced for or against E.T.

Yours ever Edward Thomas

'Home'

Hare Hall Camp, 7 and 10 March 1916

Fair was the morning, fair our tempers, and
We had seen nothing fairer than that land,
Though strange, and the untrodden snow that made
Wild of the tame, casting out all that was
Not wild and rustic and old; and we were glad.

Fair too was afternoon, and first to pass
Were we that league of snow, next the north wind.

There was nothing to return for except need.
And yet we sang nor ever stopped for speed,
As we did often with the start behind.
Faster still strode we when we came in sight
Of the cold roofs where we must spend the night.

Happy we had not been there, nor could be,
Though we had tasted sleep and food and fellowship
Together long.
           'How quick' to someone's lip
The word came, 'will the beaten horse run home.'

The word 'home' raised a smile in us all three,
And one repeated it, smiling just so
That all knew what he meant and none would say.
Between three counties far apart that lay
We were divided and looked strangely each
At the other, and we knew we were not friends
But fellows in a union that ends
With the necessity for it, as it ought.

Never a word was spoken, not a thought
Was thought, of what the look meant with the word
'Home' as we walked and watched the sunset blurred.
And then to me the word, only the word,
'Homesick', as it were playfully occurred:
No more. If I should ever more admit
Than the mere word I could not endure it
For a day longer: this captivity

Must somehow come to an end, else I should be
Another man, as often now I seem,
Or this life be only an evil dream.

Letters to Eleanor Farjeon and Robert Frost, 27 February and 5 March 1916

The conversation about homesickness and the description of the weather and living conditions in camp in the Farjeon letter are reflected in the poem. The Frost letter also describes living conditions in camp as well as the walk that the poem celebrates. The comment 'yesterday I rhymed some' refers to the composition of 'Celandine'. In a second letter to Frost on 21 May 1916 Thomas confirms the autobiographical origins of ' 'Home' ', describing various of his soldier companions including Paul Nash, and observing 'I am really lucky to have such a crowd of people always round & these 2 or 3 nearer: you might guess from "Home" how much nearer.'

Hut 16, Sunday,
My dear Eleanor   postmarked Romford, 27 February 1916

How nice to go to Coldwaltham (nicer to up Waltham). We are kept much indoors by weather unsuitable for mapping. This is Sunday a wet thawing Sunday and not really a holiday but just a day when few know what to do unless they are on leave. Somebody said something about homesickness the other day. It is a disease one can suppress but not do without under these conditions.

We are all in a turmoil of speculations. We are to have a new (and worse) sergeant major. The instructors are to be shuffled about and some (I expect) to go. Men over 30, they say, are to be transferred to fighting units as unfit for officers.

I can't write a bit. I am restless till I can. Can you and do you, in the snow? I am hoping everyone will clear out of the hut soon and leave me alone. The snow is all dirty again and I can't walk alone here and nobody wants to walk. You will have Helen down when this comes perhaps.

You will both be at Steep this day week, I hope. But I already begin to see it will be an absurdly short day. Measles, too, may intervene. There are many new cases today and only this hut has entirely escaped in our company. I am quite well again and unable not to take a cold bath.

It's snowing again now. 'Is the canteen open?' is the cry. I must make some tea.

Goodbye. I must end this and allow myself to get so bored that I must write something or go out.

Tell Helen I shall write to her tomorrow. She should have had a letter before she left home and I hope she did.

Yours ever
Edward Thomas

My dear Robert,   Hare Hall Camp, 5 March [1916]

No one can have Patience who pursues Glory, so you will have to toss up with Eleanor which vice you shall claim in public.

Well, I was hoping your silence meant you had something better to do than writing letters. When they told me you would contribute to the Annual I thought it likely. Now I am glad to hear it is so, but sorry to have to wait for the Annual before seeing the poems. I don't know if you got them, but I have sent several from time to time. Your not mentioning them made me think I had missed fire. I have written so many I suppose I am always missing fire.

I have done nothing like your lecture at Lawrence. As soon as I stand up & look at 30 men I can do nothing but crawl backwards & forwards between the few points I can still remember under the strain. It will mean a long war if I am to improve. You ask if I think it is going to be a long war. I don't think, but I do expect a lot of unexpected things & am not beginning really to look forward to any change. I hardly go beyond assuming that the war will end.

We have been through a time of change here lately. In fact we may not be out of it yet. I was not sure if the reconstruction would have me out & compel me to take a commission. Today it seems more likely we shall go on as we were. Even so, if I have to wait much longer for promotion I shall be inclined to throw this job up. I have been restless lately. Partly the annoyance of my promotion being delayed. Partly the rain and the long hours indoors. Partly my 10 days chill. Then there has been measles in the camp for 6 weeks and now we have it and are isolated and denied our leave this week, which includes my birthday when I meant to be at Steep.

This should only improve what you condemn as my fastidious taste in souls. Yet soul is a word I feel I can't have used for years & years. Anyhow here I have to like people because they are more my sort than others, although I realise at certain times they are not my sort at all & will vanish away after the war. What almost completes the illusion is that I can't help talking to them as if they were friends.

Partly what made me restless was the desire to write, without the power. It lasted 5 or 6 weeks till yesterday I rhymed some.

Your talking of epic and play rather stirred me. I shall be careful not to *indulge* in a spring run of lyrics. I had better try again to make other people speak. I suppose I take it easily, especially now when it is partly an indulgence – I wish you would send some of yours without bargaining.

Well, the long & short of it seems to be that I am what I was, in spite of my hopes of last July. The only thing is perhaps I didn't quite know what I was. This less active life you see gives me more time & inclination to ruminate. Also it is Sunday, always a dreary ruminating day if spent in camp. We got a walk, three of us, one a schoolmaster, the other a game-breeder who knows about horses & dogs & ferrets. We heard the first blackbird, walked 9 or 10 miles straight across country (the advantage of our uniform – we go just where we like): ate & drank (stout) by a fire at a big quiet inn – not a man to drink left in the village: drew a panorama – a landscape for military purposes drawn exactly with the help of a compass & a protractor, which is an amusement I have quite taken to – they say I am a neo-realist at it.

Abercrombie wrote a nice letter about some of my verses he had seen. Nobody's compliments would *flatter* me so much or more.

I can't go on with this now because everything is upside down. We don't know who or where or what we are. We five don't want to be split up & scattered. On the other hand we may each be made independent & put in charge of a company & so get rapid promotion.

Goodbye. They are all well at home, & Mervyn at Coventry. I was to have gone home for my birthday last week. Eleanor Farjeon was there. Now I have a chance of going this week end. My presents are waiting for me. But one of the best things I had on the day was your letter – a lucky accident. Give my love to them all & I hope I shall see them before I am still another year older.

Yours ever
Edward Thomas

Thaw

Over the land freckled with snow half-thawed
The speculating rooks at their nests cawed
And saw from elm-tops, delicate as flower of grass,
What we below could not see, Winter pass.

Letter to Robert Frost, 16 March 1916

The description of conditions in camp in this letter reflects the
scene painted in 'Thaw'. Thomas also discusses 'Rain'.

My dear Robert   Hare Hall Camp, 16 March 1916

Your letter of February 24 only reached me yesterday. It referred to
some verses I had sent – dismal ones, I gather. Perhaps one was called
'Rain', a form of excrement you hoped it was when you said 'work
all that off in poetry & I shan't complain'. Well, I never know. I was
glad to know of a letter reaching you. I had begun to fear perhaps my
letters didn't reach you. Lately I was able to write again. But I got
home on Saturday & left them there. If I can find the rough draft here
I will copy one out.

Things are still difficult here. There has been a complete reorgan-
isation. We do not know how it will affect us ultimately. So far it has
meant that we only instruct the company (D) to which we have been
attached since Xmas, whereas we used to instruct the whole battalion
of 4 companies in turn. Our sergeant has gone, left us, so the corporal
who would have been my junior is now in charge of us & may get
made a sergeant & leave me still as I was. We are very busy. I lecture
twice a day. Nearly all the work is indoors, & the weather is changing
at last. The snow has melted. The sun is very warm. The rooks in the
camp trees are nesting. They wake us at 5.30. We turn out for phys-
ical drill at 6.30. I have made myself fire-lighter now. We are 4
non-commissioned officers in one hut & N.C.O.'s are not supposed
to do anything menial, which is hard on the other men, there being
usually only one N.C.O. in a hut of 25 or 30. So to appease them I
light the 2 stoves while they are in bed, & so far the Lord has been on
my side, my fires are wonderful. That is where my modesty fails, you
perceive.

Yes I knew it was a year ago you went away, & two since Tyler's

Green; – & one before what? But Ledington, my dear Robert, in April, in June, in August.

It *is* warm today. We have a day with no work (but plenty to consider) & 2 of us are left in the parlour of 'The Shepherd & Dog' 2 miles from camp, a public house rather like that one at Tyler's Green or Penn. I am writing this & the other man, who is an artist, is trying to draw me. The taproom is very noisy, but here there is only a fire & 3 billiard balls on a table & us. He is the man through whom I fell into disgrace. I haven't outlived it yet. But now there is a chance my senior *may* go to another company & leave me in charge of D. The worst of it is he & I are very good pals and if we are in different companies we can't see nearly so much of one another. This means a lot because most of the men around are going to be officers soon & fresh ones will arrive & take their places & then still another set arrive.

You might have sent me Flint's address. I hardly know where to find it, unless through Monro.

I heard from de la Mare lately. He has been talking to Newbolt about a pension for me. Newbolt he says isn't very hopeful.

When I was at home I picked out 40 poems & sent them to Bottomley to pick out as many as he likes to fill 15 or 20 pages.

The news nowadays is pretty good. It looks as if we could stand any battering the Germans inflict & as if we might yet give them a battering they could not stand. There is a prophecy abroad that it will be over by July 17. Helen says Why not by her birthday, which is a few days earlier? She would be more pleased than I. She has had enough of the war & of comparative solitude

———

Well, we had to leave the inn (being soldiers) at 2.30. We drew a panorama (you must see some some day) & got back to the usual thing & the news that my brother has got his 2nd stripe on his sleeve, i.e. is a full corporal. These reminders that I am going to be passed over all the time don't please me, especially at the end of a soft moist warm day, the first such day since last April. But I am yours ever
Edward Thomas

If I Should Ever by Chance [1 Bronwen]

'At Little Warley and Hare Hall',
29 March–6 April 1916

If I should ever by chance grow rich
I'll buy Codham, Cockridden, and Childerditch,
Roses, Pyrgo, and Lapwater,
And let them all to my elder daughter.
The rent I shall ask of her will be only
Each year's first violets, white and lonely,
The first primroses and orchises –
She must find them before I do, that is.
But if she finds a blossom on furze
Without rent they shall all for ever be hers,
Codham, Cockridden, and Childerditch,
Roses, Pyrgo and Lapwater, –
I shall give them all to my elder daughter.

W.H. Davies, 'Days that have Been', *Songs of Joy* (London: A.C. Fifield, 1911)

Thomas praised this poem in his 30 January 1912 *Daily Chronicle* review of *Songs of Joy* for its 'exquisite music of some old Monmouthshire names that were sweet, but never so sweet'. 'If I Should Ever by Chance' echoes Davies's poem with its own list of Essex names.

Can I forget the sweet days that have been,
    When poetry first began to warm my blood;
When from the hills of Gwent I saw the earth
    Burned into two by Severn's silver flood:

When I would go alone at night to see
    The moonlight, like a big white butterfly,
Dreaming on that old castle near Caerleon,
    While at its side the Usk went softly by:

When I would stare at lovely clouds in Heaven,
    Or watch them when reported by deep streams;
When feeling pressed like thunder, but would not
    Break into that grand music of my dreams?

Can I forget the sweet days that have been,
　The villages so green I have been in;
Llantarnam, Magor, Malpas, and Llanwern,
　Liswery, old Caerleon, and Alteryn?

Can I forget the banks of Malpas Brook,
　Or Ebbw's voice in such a wild delight,
As on he dashed with pebbles in his throat,
　Gurgling towards the sea with all his might?

Ah, when I see a leafy village now,
　I sigh and ask it for Llantarnam's green;
I ask each river where is Ebbw's voice –
　In memory of the sweet days that have been.

Letter to Eleanor Farjeon, 1 March 1916

Thomas reveals his fascination for 'Cockridden' as a potential rhyme. He also expresses a sense of nostalgia and growing lack of liberty, feelings that may have influenced the valedictory tone of the four poems addressed respectively to his three children and to his wife ('If I Should Ever by Chance', 'If I were to Own', 'What Shall I Give' and 'And You, Helen') that together he termed the 'household poems'.

My dear Eleanor   Hut 14, Wednesday

If you are back on Friday this will find you at Hampstead. It is chiefly to say I very much hope to go home again on Saturday & to see you on the way. As you probably can't answer in time I will come to Shearn's as soon after 1 as I can on Saturday. Nothing is certain here but I am promised leave. There are more chances of leave this week than there are men expecting it, so I step into an extra chance, or hope to.

Dillybrook is like Cockridden no less because it isn't in a rhyme. But it would have been nice to have another Spring with you. Nice even to think of here where we are losing more and more of our liberty. We had a walk this afternoon – Wednesday always is a ½ holiday. Thursday used to be a holiday for us while the rest did engineering. Now we may be landed.

I have leisure to feel what I am missing. Still I don't miss everything – and what did I ever do more than not miss everything. Goodbye till Saturday.
　Yours ever
　Edward Thomas

If I were to Own [2 Merfyn]

Hare Hall, 1–7 April 1916

If I were to own this countryside
As far as a man in a day could ride,
And the Tyes were mine for giving or letting, –
Wingle Tye and Margaretting
Tye, – and Skreens, Gooshays, and Cockerells,
Shellow, Rochetts, Bandish, and Pickerells,
Martins, Lambkins, and Lillyputs,
Their copses, ponds, roads, and ruts,
Fields where plough-horses steam and plovers
Fling and whimper, hedges that lovers
Love, and orchards, shrubberies, walls
Where the sun untroubled by north wind falls,
And single trees where the thrush sings well
His proverbs untranslatable,
I would give them all to my son
If he would let me any one
For a song, a blackbird's song, at dawn.
He should have no more, till on my lawn
Never a one was left, because I
Had shot them to put them into a pie, –
His Essex blackbirds, every one,
And I was left old and alone.

Then unless I could pay, for rent, a song
As sweet as a blackbird's, and as long –
No more – he should have the house, not I:
Margeretting or Wingle Tye,
Or it might be Skreens, Gooshays, or Cockerells,
Shellow, Rochetts, Bandish, or Pickerells,
Martins, Lambkins, or Lillyputs,
Should be his till the cart tracks had no ruts.

**Eleanor Farjeon, 'Orchard Street', *Punch* (26 April 1916) and
Nursery Rhymes of London Town (London: Duckworth,
1916)**

Thomas and Eleanor Farjeon shared an interest in proverbs,
rhymes and writing for children. Thomas recognised the affinity

between her *Nursery Rhymes of London Town* and his own poetry and collection of retold proverbs, *Four-and-Twenty Blackbirds*. He calls her book 'a companion to my 4 and 20 Blackbirds' in the summer of 1915. He also says, in reference to his *Poems* in March 1917, that they will be 'bards together'. 'Orchard Street' is similar to the first three 'household' poems in its use of lists and its conditional offering of gifts. Like the blackbirds offered to Thomas's son in 'If I were to Own', the grapes in 'Orchard Street' are offered only to be withheld, 'just out of reach'.

> The fruit hangs ripe, the fruit hangs sweet,
> High and low in my Orchard Street,
> Apples and pears, cherries and plums,
> Something for every one who comes.
>> If you're a Pedlar
>> I'll give you a medlar,
>> If you're a Prince
>> I'll give you a quince,
>> If you're a Queen
>> A nectarine,
>> If you're the King
>> Take anything,
> Apricots, mulberries, melons, or red and white
> Currants like rubies and pearls on a string!
>> Little girls each
>> Shall have a peach,
> Boys shall have grapes that hang just out of reach –
> Nothing's to pay, whatever you eat
> Of the fruit that grows in my Orchard Street.

Edward Thomas's Poets

What Shall I Give [3 Myfanwy]

Hare Hall, 2-8 April 1916

What shall I give my daughter the younger
More than will keep her from cold and hunger?
I shall not give her anything.
If she shared South Weald and Havering,
Their acres, the two brooks running between,
Paine's Brook and Weald Brook,
With pewit, woodpecker, swan, and rook,
She would be no richer than the queen
Who once on a time sat in Havering Bower
Alone, with the shadows, pleasure and power.
She could do no more with Samarcand,
Or the mountains of a mountain land
And its far white house above cottages
Like Venus above the Pleiades.
Her small hands I would not cumber
With so many acres and their lumber,
But leave her Steep and her own world
And her spectacled self with hair uncurled,
Wanting a thousand little things
That time without contentment brings.

**W.H. Davies, 'Sweet Stay-at-Home', *Foliage: Various Poems*
(London: Elkin Mathews, 1913)**

> Thomas refers to this 'charming poem' in his November 1913
> *Bookman* review of *Foliage* but criticises 'the dullness and
> commonness of the phrase, "as far as eyes can go", and the dull-
> ness and looseness of two lines in his [Davies's] defence of
> "Sweet Well-Content, sweet Love-One-Place": "For thou hast
> made more homely stuff/ Nurture thy gentle self enough".'

Sweet Stay-at-Home, sweet Well-content,
Thou knowest of no strange continent:
Thou hast not felt thy bosom keep
A gentle motion with the deep;
Thou hast not sailed in Indian seas,
Where scent comes forth in every breeze.
Thou hast not seen the rich grape grow

For miles, as far as eyes can go;
Thou hast not seen a summer's night
When maids could sew by a worm's light;
Nor the North Sea in spring send out
Bright hues that like birds flit about
In solid cages of white ice –
Sweet Stay-at-Home, sweet Love-one-place.
Thou hast not seen black fingers pick
White cotton when the bloom is thick,
Nor heard black throats in harmony;
Nor hast thou sat on stones that lie
Flat on the earth, that once did rise
To hide proud kings from common eyes;
Thou hast not seen plains full of bloom
Where green things had such little room
They pleased the eye like fairer flowers –
Sweet Stay-at-Home, all these long hours.
Sweet Well-content, sweet Love-one-place,
Sweet, simple maid, bless thy dear face;
For thou hast made more homely stuff
Nurture thy gentle self enough;
I love thee for a heart that's kind –
Not for the knowledge in thy mind.

And You, Helen *[4 Helen]*

Hare Hall, 9 April 1916

And you, Helen, what should I give you?
So many things I would give you
Had I an infinite great store
Offered me and I stood before
To choose. I would give you youth,
All kinds of loveliness and truth,
A clear eye as good as mine,
Lands, waters, flowers, wine,
As many children as your heart
Might wish for, a far better art
Than mine can be, all you have lost
Upon the travelling waters tossed,
Or given to me. If I could choose
Freely in that great treasure-house
Anything from any shelf,
I would give you back yourself,
And power to discriminate
What you want and want it not too late,
Many fair days free from care
And heart to enjoy both foul and fair,
And myself, too, if I could find
Where it lay hidden and it proved kind.

Gordon Bottomley's inscription to his poem 'A Vision of Giorgione', *Poems of Thirty Years* (London: Constable, 1925)

Bottomley's inscription to his wife, Emily, dated 1914, stands in direct contrast to the last lines of Thomas's poem to his wife, Helen.

TO MY WIFE
AN OLD GIFT AND A NEW

Where all is yours,
What virtue lies in giving?
Though nought endures,
In writing as in living
I have given myself to you;

And, as you take me,
My poems grow more true,
More true you make me.

Letter to Gordon Bottomley, 24 April 1916

While discussing selection of his poems for *An Annual of New Poetry*, Thomas alludes to the 'household poems' ('If I Should Ever by Chance', 'If I were to Own', 'What Shall I Give' and 'And You, Helen') and his plans to have them illustrated. The reference to Bottomley's wife as an amanuensis could suggest that Thomas is aware of the contrast between his own fourth 'household poem', 'And You, Helen', a muted address to his wife Helen, and Bottomley's warm dedicatory inscription to his 'A Vision of Giorgione', celebrating his wife Emily as his muse.

My dear Gordon,   Hut 3, 24 April 1916

You shall have 'Wind & Mist'. But what about 'The Glory'? Could 'After Rain' take its place? However, if you would rather not, leave the selection as it is: for after all I have only fondness to go by. 'Aspens' anyhow will have to stay out. The household poems ought perhaps to appear as a bunch. John Wheatley here is talking of doing some etchings to illustrate these & one or two other Essex things. Do you know Wheatley's work? Paul Nash I am not likely to meet unless he comes to camp here. He is with our old Sergeant Maresco Pearce in town, I gather. We might go anywhere under canvas, & I should not mind a change, though I have got to like this part very much. Soon it may be quite changed by spring excursions. Up to now it has been purely rustic, except for decrepit boards with 'teas' painted on them. Wherever we move I ought to be able to see you on one of your days. When you know (more or less) exactly which they are, will you let me know, so that I can be prepared. Perhaps I could see you at the Shiffolds. I want to see Trevelyan again, too.

I wonder what will happen to Edmund John. He has a new book coming & has been photographed in khaki. I suppose he too is a Welshman like Davies. Davies, it appears, succeeded in looking natural. I believe he wore a new velvet jacket, which apparently is what a bard naturally wears. The poor men in black clothes were accused of dressing up, by one paper. I have not heard a word about it from de la Mare.

I will certainly not give up the idea of coming to you in July & if it seems possible later I will let you know in time. At last we have had 2 days leave without asking for it & we all hope it means a return to the old state of things – fortnightly leave.

My love to your amanuensis

Yours ever Edward Thomas

Go now (Like the Touch of Rain)
Hare Hall, 23–30 April 1916

Like the touch of rain she was
On a man's flesh and hair and eyes
When the joy of walking thus
Has taken him by surprise:

With the love of the storm he burns,
He sings, he laughs, well I know how,
But forgets when he returns
As I shall not forget her 'Go now'.

Those two words shut a door
Between me and the blessed rain
That was never shut before
And will not open again.

Lascelles Abercrombie, 'All Last Night…', *Interludes and Poems* (London: John Lane, 1908)

This poem appears to inform both 'Go now' and 'It Rains'. Thomas reviewed *Interludes and Poems* for the *Daily Chronicle* (29 February 1908). On 26 February 1908, he wrote to Bottomley that Abercrombie 'has his own vocabulary & a wonderful variety in his blank verse, has certainly his own vision of things'.

All last night I had quiet
In a fragrant dream and warm:
She had become my Sabbath,
And round my neck, her arm.

I knew the warmth in my dreaming;
The fragrance, I suppose,
Was her hair about me,
Or else she wore a rose.

Her hair, I think; for likest
Woodruffe 'twas, when Spring
Loitering down wet woodways
Treads it sauntering.

No light, nor any speaking;
Fragrant only and warm.
Enough to know my lodging,
The white Sabbath of her arm.

Letter to Eleanor Farjeon, 8 May 1916

Thomas's reference to 'Go now' also alludes to his enjoyment
of the associated weather conditions. There is a suggestion that
the weather, sensory delight in it and the act of composition are
connected, especially since the poem places a similar focus on
the sensation of rain and the joy of walking. The poem's image
of a door closing also suggests such an interpretation, since this
image is frequently used by Thomas in his writings to refer to
the act of poetic composition. Like the poem, the letter alludes
to lost opportunities in its emphasis on the uncertainties in
Thomas's life at this time.

My dear Eleanor,   Hut 3, Thursday, postmarked 8 May 1916

There is no hurry about the verses. I hope you like some of them
better when you see them again. Somehow I thought 2 or 3 of them
were all right, particularly 'Go now' perhaps. They are the last I have
written. This fine warm weather has given me enough to do enjoying
it. Last week we wasted too much time to enjoy it as much as I wanted
to, though we had 3 good long walks. This week has been busier and
the intervals have been far pleasanter. There are nightingales all
round the camp. The may has been out more than a week. There
have been glorious warm still evenings.

No news, except that Benson and Mason have gone to other
companies, and Vernon and I are left to work with D. The worst of
it is he is going into a billet with his wife and I am to remain (prob-
ably) in charge of this vile hut.

No hurry about Mrs Meynell. You do as you think best. De la
Mare isn't a bit hopeful, so I need all the help I can get. He doesn't
seem to think I shall have anything at all.

I doubt if anything will come of the Welsh Army job. It looks too much as if the Welsh press wanted someone to send them 'Eye-witness' stuff, which I suppose I could do, but with difficulty and not to suit Welsh taste. I only wish it would come off because it is unlikely the work here will be better organised in future, and unless it is I shall always be sick with either uncertainty or idleness.

I am expecting to go home tomorrow, perhaps just till Sunday morning, tho if the weather settles fine I may walk to Haslemere and catch the 4.20, I think it is. Is there a chance of your coming over? If I knew I was coming by the 4.20 we could meet in town *if* you are to be in town. I should have a couple of hours to spare.

Yours ever
Edward Thomas

Edward Thomas's Poets

Some eyes condemn [Sonnet 4]

'Hare Hall and train'
13 and 14 May 1916

Some eyes condemn the earth they gaze upon:
Some wait patiently till they know far more
Than earth can tell them: some laugh at the whole
As folly of another's making: one
I knew that laughed because he saw, from core
To rind, not one thing worth the laugh his soul
Had ready at waking: some eyes have begun
With laughing; some stand startled at the door.

Others, too, I have seen rest, question, roll,
Dance, shoot. And many I have loved watching. Some
I could not take my eyes from till they turned
And loving died. I had not found my goal.
But thinking of your eyes, dear, I become
Dumb: for they flamed, and it was me they burned.

**Letters to Jesse Berridge and Eleanor Farjeon, 7 November
1902 and 9 June 1916**

The reservations Thomas expresses to Berridge about the
sonnet form when discussing Berridge's *Sonnets of a Platonist*
are reflected in his reference to a 'click' in the ending of 'Some
eyes condemn' in a letter to Eleanor Farjeon fourteen years later.

My dear Jesse,   Rose Acre, 7 November 1902

I have been reading your sonnets carefully. I was struck at once by
the advance you have made since *The White Altar*. The technique
seems to me wonderfully good. There is barely a slip – except that
you rhyme 'reveal' & 'ideal' & make these words into trisyllables.
'Some spiritual haven under quiet air.' I know the line can be
defended, but it does not seem to me to be superior in music to a
normal line. The word spirit has suffered much at the hands of Milton
(who may have pronounced it 'sprite') and Tennyson; & I don't like
to see it. Another improvement is – the way in which you have
brought pauses in the sense almost invariably at the end of the line.
You used to be inclined (like many another) to ignore the end of a

line & let the sense wing on to the 2nd or 3rd syllable of a following line, with offence to harmony as well as sense. Here and there I find quite perfect lines like these – 'You breathe the roses of midsummer too, And winter's peace, & spring so much desired.' But I have made myself rather miserable by a feeling that I do not understand you sufficiently to see that there is a *sequence* of ideas or emotions in your series. And if I do not understand, you will hardly expect me to criticize. Yet I think I must say that you seem to me to have succumbed in places to the difficulties of dealing with an abstraction. In No. XXIII for example, you speak of a 'time-touched face', & I find it hard to believe that you do not mean a human face. Again, in No. XIV you say: 'Your verses found me in a happy hour...' Whose verses? (That sonnet by the way contains an ugly misprint – DANAE.)

Personally, I have a dread of the sonnet. It must contain 14 lines, & a man must be a tremendous poet or a cold mathematician if he can accommodate his thoughts to such a condition. The result is – in my opinion – that many of the best sonnets are rhetoric only. I think most of Rossetti's are. Rossetti too is responsible for introducing the sesquipedalian-word sonnet, & he might have written the line

'Philosophy's ideal incarnated.'

Sesquipedalian words are all very well & they are often magnificent – in you among others. But once under the spell, sense & concreteness are apt to disappear. That is so often in Rossetti. He expresses his emotion, if at all, by the sound of the words & not by their meaning. His sonnets are often like big men in pompous clothes. They are impressive without saying anything – and I really think you are inclined to follow him. I took you at your word, I took you as a 'Platonist' & I analysed & paraphrased several sonnets – and I think I found too little substance. I fear you will quarrel with the method. But then all of Shakespeare's will bear it. I don't mean that every sonnet should contain a fresh & striking idea that would look well in a leading article. I mean that if a sonnet fails to produce an impression of strength & unity, if, on analysis, it still seems to lack unity & strength, then it is inconsiderable.

Frankly, I think you are not quite justified in calling yourself a Platonist. That you have read and loved him there is no doubt. But that you have read all of him & thoroughly digested his work after a comparison with philosophers of other schools, I am inclined to disbelieve. For Plato's *ideas* seem to me as concrete as Goethe's *men & women* – You on the other hand conspicuously lack concreteness;

Edward Thomas's Poets

you seem to realize it yourself, & to make up for it by a blend of the real & the ideal. N.B. I use 'concrete' figuratively, to imply clearness & firmness. A Platonist, it seems to me, is one who, having mastered Plato, builds upon the foundations laid by Plato. That is, he is not a disciple so much as a successor. You, on the other hand, seem to have been content as I should do myself, i.e. to take a hint from a phrase or passage in Plato, and to let it germinate in your own brain. That is not Platonism! It is the higher plagiarism, & I know something about that.

Frankly, in the second place, I don't think the sonnet suits you – you have written sonnets that are lovely in form. But I think it encourages your aerial tendency too much. It compels you to use words loosely, to forget that words have a value beyond their sound. Thus, I think that, as far as feeling & substance go, some of your lyrics are far superior to your sonnets, simply because you have the lyrical impulse (your sonnets show it) & because you have more freedom in variable measures.

In conclusion, nothing will please me better than a proof that (1) you are a Platonist & (2) you are a born sonneteer.

Yours ever
Edward Thomas

My dear Eleanor,   9 June 1916

Thank you for your letter and the typescript. I am glad you liked the sonnet, I suppose it was one. My fear was that it ended with a click. 'One' is I suppose, a weakness.

Fancy that phrase coming in the autobiography, and fancy my not putting in the whooping cough – Helen says I did have it, but I only put down what I remembered. So I can come to see you when I have a chance next. I am so glad you aren't whooping.

They are to give me £300 instead of a pension. So I can set Mervyn up for a time. He may go to the London United Tramway Works at Walthamstow if I can arrange lodgings there. I don't like his being just anywhere and on his own with so little of his own apparently. One of my brothers thinks he can get him there as an apprentice with every chance of learning.

I do hope David will escape. I have been trying for an artillery commission but without military influence it looks as if I might have a long wait. Luckily we have been quite busy here and I have had less to complain of.

I expect to go to Steep again next week. If I have any time I will

rush up to Hampstead on my way. Or could you come out and stay
out? Is that allowed? Goodbye.

    Yours ever

    Edward Thomas

The sun used to shine

Hare Hall, 22 May 1916

The sun used to shine while we two walked
Slowly together, paused and started
Again, and sometimes mused, sometimes talked
As either pleased, and cheerfully parted

Each night. We never disagreed
Which gate to rest on. The to be
And the late past we gave small heed.
We turned from men or poetry

To rumours of the war remote
Only till both stood disinclined
For aught but the yellow flavorous coat
Of an apple wasps had undermined;

Or a sentry of dark betonies,
The stateliest of small flowers on earth,
At the forest verge; or crocuses
Pale purple as if they had their birth

In sunless Hades fields. The war
Came back to mind with the moonrise
Which soldiers in the east afar
Beheld then. Nevertheless, our eyes

Could as well imagine the Crusades
Or Caesar's battles. Everything
To faintness like those rumours fades –
Like the brook's water glittering

Under the moonlight – like those walks
Now – like us two that took them, and
The fallen apples, all the talks
And silences – like memory's sand

When the tide covers it late or soon,
And other men through other flowers
In those fields under the same moon
Go talking and have easy hours.

1916

131

Gordon Bottomley, 'In January', written 1909, in *Poems and Plays* (London: The Bodley Head, 1953)

Although set in winter, and reflecting Bottomley's experience as an invalided observer of others, the positioning of both speaker and walker in a timeless context in the last three verses of this poem resonates with the ending of 'The sun used to shine'.

O, shepherd out upon the snow,
What lambs are newly born?...
I see his long, long shadow go
Across the fields of morn.

Ere dawn the snow-light in the room
Awoke me, and I saw
A pallid earth, a cloudy gloom,
A shape that stirred my awe.

I know the clear untrodden snows
That hide the Winter wheat;
The greyer fields wherein he goes
Are grey with pitting feet.

He feels not how I watch him creep,
He thinks he is alone;
He searches for the heavy sheep
Each windward hedge of stone.

I keep my bed in weariness
When workers have gone forth,
I watch that silent man grow less
Into the snow-packed North;

And men have died in this old room
Through thrice a hundred years
Who saw the shepherd in the gloom,
The shape that never nears.

Briefly I watch; but then I go,
The room will know me not;
Yet from my window, o'er the snow,
When I am well forgot

Edward Thomas's Poets

Shall unknown men look forth to scan
Each far, unchanging tree,
And see a dark and lonely man
Still creeping agelessly.

from Edward Thomas's 'The Stile', *Light and Twilight* (London: Duckworth, 1911)

Thomas told Eleanor Farjeon on 4 June 1915 that 'The sun used to shine' is about 'Me and Frost'. However, it also carries echoes of the following passage from 'The Stile', which Thomas wrote long before he met Frost, and which is most probably based on his friendship with de la Mare, as Helen Thomas asserts in a 1940 letter to de la Mare: "'The Stile' enshrines his [Thomas's] feeling for you.'

One day I stopped by the stile at the corner to say good-bye to a friend who had walked thus far with me. It was about half an hour after the sunset of a dry, hot day among the many wet ones in that July. We had been talking easily and warmly together, in such a way that there was no knowing whose was any one thought, because we were in electrical contact and each leapt to complete the other's words, just as if some poet had chosen to use the form of an eclogue and had made us the two shepherds who were to utter his mind through our dialogue. When he spoke I had already the same thing in the same words to express. When either of us spoke we were saying what we could not have said to any other man at any other time.

But as we reached the stile our tongues and our steps ceased together, and I was instantly aware of the silence through which our walking and talking had drawn a thin line up to this point.

Walter de la Mare, 'Silence', *The Listeners* (London: Constable, 1912)

De la Mare's use of images of war as a backdrop to the communion between two friends resembles 'The sun used to shine'.

With changeful sound life beats upon the ear;
    Yet, striving for release,
    The most seductive string's
    Sweet jargonings,

1916   133

The happiest throat's
Most easeful, lovely notes
Fall back into a veiling silentness.

Ev'n 'mid the rumour of a moving host,
  Blackening the clear green earth,
  Vainly 'gainst the thin wall
    The trumpets call,
    Or with loud hum
  The smoke-bemuffled drum:
From that high quietness no reply comes forth.

When, all at peace, two friends at ease alone
  Talk out their hearts – yet still,
  Between the grace-notes of
    The voice of love
    From each to each
  Trembles a rarer speech,
And with its presence every pause doth fill.

Unmoved it broods, this all-encompassing hush
  Of one who stooping near,
  No smallest stir will make
    Our fear to wake;
    But yet intent
  Upon some mystery bent
Hearkens the lightest word we say, or hear.

Letter to Robert Frost, 19 September 1914

Thomas's summary of his *Nation* article 'This England' is
similar to elements in 'The sun used to shine'. Like the third
verse of that poem, the letter also combines references to war
with a mention of apples.

My dear Frost,   Steep, 19 September 1914

Sew-and-sew is good.
  Your letter came when my hands were full of a man full of
platichewds, with whom I was bicycling off (on Thursday) for a night
near the sea with James Guthrie an artist you've heard me speak of.
I had a good ride there & back over the Downs & a swim too in a cold

rough sea rather. But I am tired after it & have only been able to type & add a little rather dully to an article on the new moon of August 26 & you & me strolling about in the sun while our brave soldiers &c. I doubt if I shall get nearer soldiering than I did then, chiefly for fear of leaving many tangles behind & not being able to make any new ones for perhaps a long time. So I probably shall see you before the year's old. I might go to Wales & to you on the way back. But I might just see if there is any paid work to do. I did my English review article & have just corrected the proof. Your suggestion for others I scorn. Earning a living is a serious business.

We are losing Bronwen again this term. She got to London on Tuesday with her cousiness who is here now. Mervyn for lack of anything better goes to school as usual probably. I don't think any of us will go to Ellis'. It is not convenient to leave this house & my papers &c. to the damps of winter & I don't want to be alone in it with only too free a course. I could go on with the autobiography but I mightn't. Is it worth while adding the little things that crop up from time to time which I have omitted? As it is an *accumulation*. Perhaps I ought to. Your opinion relieves me, even more. I hope you will lay your finger on anything that strikes you as incomplete or dubious.

I shall be glad if I hear Mrs Nutt has got a job for you & Mrs Gardner a cottage I can cycle or walk to this autumn & winter. Next week or the week after I shall be in town & I suppose you may possibly be there too. But is Edinburgh off?

Will you send Harriet something? The Spider on the war? or philo-progenitiveness &c. Kitchener to please Mrs Gardner? I want to see her daughter, by the way.

There are some apples about here. So come if you can. And our damsons are still a sight both on the trees & in our biggest bowls. We have picked some blackberries, too. I wonder if you have ever seen the hop picking & smelt the kilns?

We had a man here a couple of nights [ago] who has been living near Keene in New Hampshire, is returning there & wants to take Mervyn. He was a schoolmaster here but talks of blacksmithing out there & would like us to be at hand. Is Keene near any part you had thought of?

I've had a compliment from Australia on the Pursuit of Spring. Otherwise I am as before and

Yours ever

E.T.

Our love to you all & I wish you were all within reach this side or the other side of the Downs.

Bugle Call (No One Cares Less than I)
Hare Hall, 25 and 26 May 1916

'No one cares less than I,
Nobody knows but God
Whether I am destined to lie
Under a foreign clod'
Were the words I made to the bugle call in the morning.

But laughing, storming, scorning,
Only the bugles know
What the bugles say in the morning,
And they do not care, when they blow
The call that I heard and made words to early this morning.

Letters to J.W. Haines and Robert Frost, 5 May and 13 June 1915 (extracts)

These extracts reveal Thomas's thoughts on Rupert Brooke's poetry, casting light on his decision, in the first lines of 'Bugle Call', to parody Brooke's opening to his 1914 poem 'The Soldier':

> If I should die, think only this of me:
> That there's some corner of a foreign field
> That is for ever England.

The discussion of Frost's 'Two Roads' ('The Road Not Taken') extracted from a very long letter to Frost serves as a contrast to the implied criticism of Brooke.

[To J.W. Haines]   Steep, 5 May 1915

I wish I knew when I could get to Gloucestershire. But I think I told you I was rather cramped and also tied entirely for fully another 2 months by a tiresome book. It is all I am doing ... It is a beautiful April, though I have been upsetting not spending any of it in your country, & only seeing it to and from my study a mile and a half away ... I have been re-reading Rupert Brooke but though his death makes certain sonnets stand out they still seem to me rather eloquent expressions of thoughts or fancies than pure poetry; but eloquent they are in a very exceptional eager youthful style.

         Edward Thomas's Poets

My dear Robert,

Your two letters came together Friday night. When I saw the Franconia postmark on the smaller I guessed it was the second – that you were there. I hope very much you still are & will be almost as long as you would like. My next hope is that I shall see you there. But this is a funny world, as I think you said before I did. 'Rum job, painting', Turner used to say when Ruskin had poured out a can of words. I wish I hadn't to say more about poetry. I wished it on Friday night particularly as I had to spoil the effect of your letter by writing 1000 words about Rupert Brooke's posthumous book – not daring to say that those sonnets about him enlisting are probably not very personal but a nervous attempt to connect with himself the very widespread idea that self sacrifice is the highest self indulgence. You know. And I don't dispute it. Only I doubt if he knew it or would he have troubled to drag in the fact that enlisting cleared him of

All the little emptiness of love?

Well, I daren't say so, not having enlisted or fought the keeper. But I ought to write about The Road not Taken. I ought to search for the poem first among your letters. But I shan't yet. I am pretty tired. I must own though that it wasn't a very honest remark that of mine. For whether it was that I was deaf or that you didn't quite speak in the verses I got the idea somewhat apart from the words. That is to say I thought I did, – the fact being that I got the idea as much as if I had skimmed the words, which I don't think I did. So at the time I was content to deceive you by referring to the poem when it was really to that idea not yet in the form of poetry which existed in my head after reading. The word 'staggering' I expect did no more than express (or conceal) the fact that the simple words and unemphatic rhythms were not such as I was accustomed to expect great things, things I like, from. It staggered me to think that perhaps I had always missed what made poetry poetry if it was here. I wanted to think it was here.

***

Honest man (Marlborough used to think he was honest), I have found 'Two Roads'. It is as I thought. Not then having begun to write I did not know that is how it would be done. It was just its newness, not like Shelley or de la Mare or anyone. I don't pretend not to have a regular road & footpath system as well as doing some trespassing. On looking at it again I complain only of a certain periphrastic loose-ness in 'the passing there had gone to them both about the same'. Also I hope that so far [you] have not found that you had to sigh on real-ising it had made all the difference, though it had. You don't wish you been Drinkwater. Another trifle – the lack of stops I believe put me off a little. There. If I say more I shall get into those nooks you think I like. It is all very well for you poets in a wood to say you choose, but you don't. If you do, ergo I am no poet. I didn't choose my sex yet I was simpler then. And so I cant 'leave off' going in after myself tho some day I may. I didn't know when I left you at Newent I was going to begin trying to write poetry. I had proved it was impossible.

***

I read 'The road not taken' to Helen just now; she liked it entirely & agreed with me how naturally symbolic it was. You won't go exag-gerate what I say about that one phrase.

This moment a letter from Haines telling me I am free to drop in on him next week as I hope to do. The weather keeps so fine though that each day it seems must be the last – just like last year.

People are getting pretty black about the war, realising they have not got the Germans beaten yet. It is said however that we are really through the Dardenelles & the price of wheat is falling. It is said to be kept back to prevent rowdyism in the rejoicing.

Good luck to you at Franconia & all our loves to you six.

Yours ever

E. Thomas

Edward Thomas's Poets

Song [3] (Early One Morning)

Hare Hall, 8–11 June 1916

Early one morning in May I set out,
And nobody I knew was about.
    I'm bound away for ever
    Away somewhere, away for ever.

There was no wind to trouble the weathercocks.
I had burnt my letters and darned my socks.

No one knew I was going away,
I thought myself I should come back some day.

I heard the brook through the town gardens run.
O sweet was the mud turned to dust by the sun.

A gate banged in a fence and banged in my head.
'A fine morning, sir,' a shepherd said.

I could not return from my liberty,
To my youth and my love and my misery.

The past is the only dead thing that smells sweet,
The only sweet thing that is not also fleet.
    I'm bound away for ever,
    Away somewhere, away for ever.

Letter to Eleanor Farjeon, 24 June 1916

'Early One Morning' is based on the song 'Rio Grande'. An early draft included the following refrain and verses:

One Friday morning in May I set out
Away for ever
It was early and no one I knew was about.

Then away somewhere Away for ever
For I'm bound to leave the old town

and:

She was lovely and young and her father unkind.
She could wait but I was hasty inclined.

She was all I missed of what I left there
No one else was so kind as none was so fair

My dear Eleanor   Tuesday, Hut 14, postmarked 24 June 1916

Look what I have done. I have been 3 days sick and confined to the camp, practically to the hut and this is the result, I have altered Rio because I feel you are right. I have cut out the 3rd and 4th verses and the only refrain is

> 'I'm bound away for ever
> Away somewhere, away for ever'

Does that do it any good?

I am better now and just going out for the first time and hope I can get a walk tomorrow and be fit on Monday.

There are more changes ahead and in case I should be robbed of it I am trying to arrange my leave to begin next Saturday. I have got to move my books from the study. Mrs Lupton has turned me out. After that Helen and I are going to the Guthries, the Ellis's, and finishing up in London. If you were at Greatham we could call there. I suppose there is a place to put up at. Otherwise we should see you in town.

It is most satisfactory that Duckworth has altered his terms in the right direction.

I remember when all the animals in the Zoo seemed to be in the moon. They were all roaring and howling together under a rising full moon while we were doing night operations in Regents Park last summer. I thought it was some horrible mob. I wonder what your baby did see there.

Goodbye. Yours ever
Edward Thomas

There was a time

There was a time when this poor frame was whole
And I had youth and never another care,
Or none that should have troubled a strong soul.
Yet, except sometimes in a frosty air
When my heels hammered out a melody
From pavements of a city left behind,
I never would acknowledge my own glee
Because it was less mighty than my mind
Had dreamed of. Since I could not boast of strength
Great as I wished, weakness was all my boast.
I sought yet hated pity till at length
I earned it. Oh, too heavy was the cost.
But now that there is something I could use
My youth and strength for, I deny the age,
The care and weakness that I know – refuse
To admit I am unworthy of the wage
Paid to a man who gives up eyes and breath
For what can neither ask nor heed his death.

Letter to Eleanor Farjeon, 29 June 1916

This letter is interesting for its revelation of the mood in which
Thomas wrote the 'longest' poems mentioned – 'There was a
time'. The letter also refers to 'Bob's Lane' ('Women he loved')
and the sonnet 'It was upon'. The 'latest' is 'The Green Roads',
and the end of this letter hints at its setting.

My dear Eleanor

Hut 14, Wednesday
postmarked 29 June 1916

I wish you were well. It is a long time since you were. Is the war
preying on you or do you write like that because you are out of tune?
I wish you could shut your eyes to many big things as I do without
trying. If they do prey on me I don't know it. But then I wasn't in a
bad mood when I wrote those lines you thought sick – I think you
meant the longest of those 3. I thought it was more than a shade
heroic. Bob's Lane I liked, but I am glad you liked the sonnet.
    About seeing you, can Helen and I see you at lunch on Thursday

next week? We hope to reach town on Wednesday night. But it might be Wednesday morning – would Wednesday lunch suit you better? Will you write to Helen and tell her which day and whether 1 at the Strand *Cottage* would do? I only get from Saturday to Thursday 9.45. We shall have to modify to suit the weather as we can't carry anything. How I wish we could fish on the way!

This is the latest. A wet warm free afternoon. The forest is a fragment left 6 miles from here, the best of all this county. I go there every time I can. There is a cottage not far off where you might like to stay some day. The people have been there 53 years. You can't imagine a wilder quieter place. Goodbye.

Yours ever
Edward Thomas

Edward Thomas's Poets

The Green Roads

Hare Hall, 28 June 1916

The green roads that end in the forest
Are strewn with white goose feathers this June,

Like marks left behind by some one gone to the forest
To show his track. But he has never come back.

Down each green road a cottage looks at the forest.
Round one the nettle towers; two are bathed in flowers.

An old man along the green road to the forest
Strays from one, from another a child alone.

In the thicket bordering the forest,
All day long a thrush twiddles his song.

It is old, but the trees are young in the forest,
All but one like a castle keep, in the middle deep.

That oak saw the ages pass in the forest:
They were a host, but their memories are lost,

For the tree is dead: all things forget the forest
Excepting perhaps me, when now I see

The old man, the child, the goose feathers at the edge of the forest,
And hear all day long the thrush repeat his song.

Walter de la Mare, 'The Dwelling-Place', *The Listeners*
(London: Constable, 1912)

> Many elements of this poem resonate with 'The Green Roads',
> and the last four verses also strike a chord with Thomas's 'Out
> in the dark'. Other de la Mare poems that bear comparison with
> 'The Green Roads' are 'The Journey' in *The Listeners*, and 'A
> Song of Enchantment' in *Peacock Pie*.

> Deep in a forest where the kestrel screamed,
>   Beside a lake of water, clear as glass,

The time-worn windows of a stone house gleamed
    Named only 'Alas'.

Yet happy as the wild birds in the glades
    Of that green forest, thridding the still air
With low continued heedless serenades,
    Its heedless people were.

The throbbing chords of violin and lute,
    The lustre of lean tapers in dark eyes,
Fair colours, beauteous flowers, faint-bloomed fruit
    Made earth seem Paradise

To them that dwelt within this lonely house:
    Like children of the gods in lasting peace,
They ate, sang, danced, as if each day's carouse
    Need never pause, nor cease.

Some might cry, Vanity! to a weeping lyre,
    Some in that deep pool mock their longings vain,
Came yet at last long silence to the wire,
    And dark did dark remain.

Some to the hunt would wend, with hound and horn,
    And clash of silver, beauty, bravery, pride,
Heeding not one who on white horse upborne
    With soundless hoofs did ride.

Dreamers there were who watched the hours away
    Beside a fountain's foam. And in the sweet
Of phantom evening, 'neath the night-bird's lay,
    Did loved with loved-one meet.

All, all were children, for, the long day done,
    They barred the heavy door against lightfoot fear;
And few words spake though one known face was gone,
    Yet still seemed hovering near.

They heaped the bright fire higher; poured dark wine;
    And in long revelry dazed the questioning eye;
Curtained three-fold the heart-dismaying shine
    Of midnight streaming by.

Edward Thomas's Poets

They shut the dark out from the painted wall,
  With candles dared the shadow at the door,
Sang down the faint reiterated call
  Of those who came no more.

Yet clear above the portal plain was writ,
  Confronting each at length alone to pass
Out of its beauty into night star-lit,
  That worn 'Alas!'

Letter to Walter de la Mare, 15 May 1912

This letter records Thomas's response to de la Mare's book *The Listeners* and in particular to 'The Dwelling-Place'.

My dear de la Mare,   Dillybrook Farm, Road nr Bath,
                                                       15 May 1912

Thank you. I have just looked through your book & am half glad half sorry, but more glad. Sorry to think there are so many poems in it I might have seen all these months: glad to think there are so many new ones to read. You won't suspect me of these dull injurious compliments when I confess I have only glanced at the book. The fact is I am writing Swinburne & can't get free just yet so I shall leave the book to fit in this evening. You won't mind hearing that Bax admired Miss Loo (& some that I believe you have left out, from the English Review) without being advised to. He lives 8 miles away and I spent Saturday night there. This is delicious country in the sun & now today in misty rain. There is may and nightingales at hand. I wish you would come. I can give you a bed and I believe I could manage Whitsun if you could. Tell me. Otherwise I may not be in town for another month. I am not sure. I am restless here now that I am writing. Many thanks for Saintsbury but to tell the truth I really can't read him, so I find now. The other book was G.M. Trevelyan's Garibaldi book or rather his 2 Italian books. If you could send them this week they would be useful, but don't trouble to send them later. When I come to town I shall be very glad to come to you if Dick doesn't mind. You aren't 40 already are you? No I wasn't too tired (for myself).

Hodgson will be pleased to see The Cherry Trees again. I am jealous of you for being able to write such unprofitable things, unprofitable even for me this time for no one has sent it to me to review. I shall have pleasure without profit for the first time in reading you.

With my love to you all and tell me if perhaps you could come.
Yours ever
E.T.

After all I stayed in in the rain I find I have read nearly all your book. You might as well ask me to write a poem myself as to write about them. Each one takes me a little deeper into a world I know just for the moment as well as you – only not really knowing it I cannot write. I think it is equal to 'Songs of Childhood' and 'Poems'. It is as fresh as the first and it has the grace of the second book like gossamer over its blossom colours. I did not think one book could be so good. My favourite is 'The Dwelling Place', if I dare commit myself.

John Freeman, 'Revisitation', *Stone Trees* (London: Selwyn and Blount, 1916)

In an April 1916 letter to Freeman, Thomas records liking 'Revisitation'. His 'The Green Roads', written two months later, presents an odd reversal of 'Revisitation''s conceit.

It is here – the lime-tree in the garden path,
The lilac by the wall, the ivied wall
That was so high, the heavy, close-leaved creeper,
The harsh gate jarring on its hinges still,
The echoing clean flags – all
The same, the same, and never more the same.

That mound was once a hill,
The old lime-tree a forest (now as small
As the poor lilac by the ivied wall),
And this neglected narrow greenery
A wilderness, and I its king and keeper;
Lying upon the grass I saw the sky
And all its clouds: the garden edged the sky.

The harsh gate jars upon its hinges still.

Letter to John Freeman, April 1916

My dear Freeman,   Hut 3, Romford, April 1916

Many thanks for your poems – the book & the typescript. I am afraid I shall be very disappointing about them. The first half of the week we were upset in our work, and the second half I was anxious about my application for leave. I dipped here & there and liked 'Revisitation', but it is the old story, they mostly are not for me. I don't begin to get into touch with them. I can't learn the language, I don't like saying so, but there is no way out if I wanted a way. Don't give me another chance of annoying you as this must annoy you, & believe me I am very sorry.

I asked about your glasses but the people at the Orange Tree had not seen them.

Yours ever,
Edward Thomas

The Swifts (How at Once)
Hospital, Hare Hall, 10 August 1916

How at once should I know,
When stretched in the harvest blue
I saw the swift's black bow,
That I would not have that view
Another day
Until next May
Again it is due?

The same year after year –
But with the swift alone.
With other things I but fear
That they will be over and done
Suddenly
And I only see
Them to know them gone.

Letters to Eleanor Farjeon, 20 August 1916 and undated

These letters reveal Thomas's preparations for moving house
while he was writing his poem about the swifts' departure. In
the first letter, Thomas, praising Eleanor Farjeon's *Nursery
Rhymes of London Town*, emphasises the role of surprise in
poetry.

My dear Eleanor   Steep, Monday [20 August 1916]

I have been here since Friday night and go tomorrow. Most of the
time I have been preparing for the move, burning books and papers
and packing boxes of books I decided I would sell. I could almost sell
the lot. At intervals we have been out and I have read some of your
poems. They are like china shepherdesses &c. They all surprise, but
not too much, just enough to make one wish one had invented them
oneself – the slut Kensal, for example. And yet I can hardly read
except what I have to, such as Gunnery Formulae simplified. I do
look forward to the new work. It is likely to begin about the end of
the month; whether at St John's Wood or not is quite uncertain. You
go roaming about. I hope it is as pleasant as it sounds. Did you chance
on Bronwen in a caravan near Littlehampton. Hardly, perhaps. She

Edward Thomas's Poets

is thereabouts for a week. Helen doesn't know where she is going.

Don't you worry about typing those 2 verses, in which I have changed 'August blue' to 'harvest blue'. I was glad to have them to write anyway – shall be lucky to do more till the swifts are back again. If I go to St John's Wood or Handel St do you think I could work at Fellows Rd of an evening? We all get sleeping out passes and can come in at midnight or for the morning parade. I go on Wednesday to look for cottages near Chigwell &c.

Goodbye and good fishing to you.

Yours ever

Edward Thomas

My dear Eleanor   Wednesday, R.A. School, Handel St, WC

Thank you for sending me the estimate and for getting it. I wrote at once proposing Sept 21 tho Goodness knows if Helen can manage it then. She says they have had some good weather. Mervyn remains silent.

I meant to come over tonight, but an arrangement for tomorrow night had to be altered, so I hope I shall find you in tomorrow night instead.

By the way, you misread that poem you didn't much like – about the swifts – missing the point that year after year I see them, *realising that it is the last time*, i.e. just before they go away for the winter (early in August). Perhaps it is too much natural history.

Yours ever

Edward Thomas

Blenheim Oranges (Gone, Gone Again)

Royal Artillery School,
Handel St, WC,
27 August 1916

Gone, gone again,
May, June, July,
And August gone,
Again gone by,

Not memorable
Save that I saw them go,
As past the empty quays
The rivers flow.

And now again,
In the harvest rain,
The Blenheim oranges
Fall grubby from the trees,

As when I was young –
And when the lost one was here –
And when the war began
To turn young men to dung.

Look at the old house,
Outmoded, dignified,
Dark and untenanted,
With grass growing instead

Of the footsteps of life,
The friendliness, the strife;
In its beds have lain
Youth, love, age and pain:

I am something like that;
Only I am not dead,
Still breathing and interested
In the house that is not dark: –

I am something like that:
Not one pane to reflect the sun,
For the schoolboys to throw at –
They have broken every one.

Walter de la Mare, 'The Song of the Secret', *Peacock Pie* (London: Constable, 1913)

The subject-matter of 'Blenheim Oranges' and 'The Song of the Secret' is similar. Both draw on images of incipient autumn to express the impermanence of beauty and both make use of the refrain 'gone, gone'. Interestingly, in his *Times Literary Supplement* review of Thomas's *Poems* (18 October 1917), de la Mare quotes directly from 'Blenheim Oranges'.

Where is beauty?
    Gone, gone:
The cold winds have taken it
    With their faint moan;
The white stars have shaken it,
    Trembling down,
Into the pathless deeps of the sea:
    Gone, gone
Is beauty from me.

The clear naked flower
    Is faded and dead;
The green-leaved willow,
    Drooping her head,
Whispers low to the shade
    Of her boughs in the stream,
        Sighing a beauty
        Secret as dream.

The Trumpet

Royal Artillery Barracks, Trowbridge,
26–8 [?] September 1916

Rise up, rise up,
And, as the trumpet blowing
Chases the dreams of men,
As the dawn glowing
The stars that left unlit
The land and water,
Rise up and scatter
The dew that covers
The print of last night's lovers –
Scatter it, scatter it!

While you are listening
To the clear horn,
Forget, men, everything
On this earth newborn,
Except that it is lovelier
Than any mysteries.
Open your eyes to the air
That has washed the eyes of the stars
Through all the dewy night:
Up with the light,
To the old wars;
Arise, arise!

Letters to Eleanor Farjeon, 25 September 1916 and undated

Royal Artillery Barracks. Trowbridge,
My dear Eleanor   Monday, postmarked 25 September 1916

It isn't bad and the weather is lovely. Moreover the Saturday and Sunday were almost free, so I walked both to Dillybrook and to Bradford by the fields. We are in tents and so we see the night sky. The trumpet blows for everything and I like that too, tho the trumpeter is not excellent. We have had our costume criticised a good deal and have had to buy gloves and so on. But it is not so bad as it was painted. I have met Hooper once or twice, in fact he was one of the Bradford party. I like him. I like men with that easy free manner better than clever men.

I may get home on Saturday tho it is an inconvenient roundabout journey by Salisbury and Portsmouth.

I hope you liked some of the verses.

Bertie did write, but of course it will be some time before I can go there now.

Are you quite well now? If so, you will be going away black-berrying or something, won't you?

Yours ever

Edward Thomas

My dear Eleanor   Wednesday

Thank you very much for everything. But I am so sleepy I don't know how much more I can say. Lectures nearly all day make me sleepy. It is rather difficult, too, to learn about pulleys and weights and the teaching is mostly almost useless. It is only 12.30 but I hardly know what I write, now or in making notes. So it is difficult to see how I shall manage it. Partly, too, the very violent physical drill explains it, and a night partly spent in trying to keep rain out of the tent. I think I told you we had some walks on Saturday and Sunday, but all the week we are practically confined to the barracks as we work till 7.30 and can't go out unless we are in our finery, which is hardly worth while changing into. However you can see I have some ease, because I have written some verses suggested by the trumpet calls which go all day. They are not well done and the trumpet is cracked, but the Reveillé pleases me (more than it does most sleepers). Here is the result. You see I have written it with only capitals to mark the lines, because people are all around me and I don't want them to know.

I like Hooper, but he is in another squad and I don't see much of him.

Yours ever

Edward Thomas

The Child in the Orchard

High Beech, October 1916

'He rolls in the orchard: he is stained with moss
And with earth, the solitary old white horse.
Where is his father and where is his mother
Among all the brown horses? Has he a brother?
I know the swallow, the hawk, and the hern;
But there are two million things for me to learn.

'Who was the lady that rode the white horse
With rings and bells to Banbury Cross?
Was there no other lady in England beside
That a nursery rhyme could take for a ride?
The swift, the swallow, the hawk, and the hern.
There are two million things for me to learn.

'Was there a man once who straddled across
The back of the Westbury White Horse
Over there on Salisbury Plain's green wall?
Was he bound for Westbury, or had he a fall?
The swift, the swallow, the hawk, and the hern.
There are two million things for me to learn.

'Out of all the white horses I know three,
At the age of six; and it seems to me
There is so much to learn, for men,
That I dare not go to bed again.
The swift, the swallow, the hawk, and the hern.
There are millions of things for me to learn.'

Letter to Eleanor Farjeon, 6 November 1916

This letter refers to 'Lights Out' (following) as well as to 'The Child in the Orchard'.

My dear Eleanor   Trowbridge, 6 November 1916

We did expect you. Baba and Mervyn and I went down some way to meet you, but we were quite prepared to be disappointed. Also we escaped drowning. They were all well, but I arrived late after being inspected by Sir William Robertson and it was more of a rush than usual.

Thank you for typing the verses. I see that 'At the age of six' is a rather rough way of explaining who speaks. But he did tell me he was six too and seemed to realise he had a long way to go. Now I have actually done still another piece which I call 'Lights Out'. It sums up what I have often thought at that call. I wish it were as brief – 2 pairs of long notes. I wonder is it nearly as good as it might be.

I am thro the exam comfortably, and now I have only 4 days more here: then a week at Wanstrow, where I suppose my address will be; 'R.G.A. Wanstrow, Somerset'. After that I shall possibly have 10 days leave. Sunday I shall spend at my Mother's. On Monday I may go to see Gordon Bottomley after some shopping; on Wednesday to High Beech. Will you come there one day? We are very full at present, having a friend of Bronwen's filling one room, or I would suggest a night or two. But I daresay I shall be in town again as there are many things to buy.

Hooper is at Wanstrow and I miss him. I saw him often last week.

I hope your Mother is better before this comes to you.

Goodbye.

Yours ever

Edward Thomas

Lights Out

Trowbridge, November 1916

I have come to the borders of sleep,
The unfathomable deep
Forest, where all must lose
Their way, however straight
Or winding, soon or late;
They can not choose.

Many a road and track
That since the dawn's first crack
Up to the forest brink
Deceived the travellers,
Suddenly now blurs,
And in they sink.

Here love ends –
Despair, ambition ends;
All pleasure and all trouble,
Although most sweet or bitter,
Here ends, in sleep that is sweeter
Than tasks most noble.

There is not any book
Or face of dearest look
That I would not turn from now
To go into the unknown
I must enter, and leave, alone,
I know not how.

The tall forest towers:
Its cloudy foliage lowers
Ahead, shelf above shelf:
Its silence I hear and obey
That I may lose my way
And myself.

Edward Thomas's Poets

Letter to Eleanor Farjeon, 2 November 1916

The letter includes a description of the conditions in which 'Lights Out' was composed.

My dear Eleanor,   Trowbridge, postmarked 2 November 1916

This is only a word to say it seems an age since I saw you or heard from you – also to send you some verses I managed to write before the end of my leave. I did something else too coming down in the train on a long dark journey when people were talking and I wasn't, but I have got it still to finish.

I had a word from Frost but only to enclose 2 photographs and say he hoped I would send him duplicates of my verses when Ingpen has made his choice, which he is slow in doing.

Now I have another exam on Saturday the last that is at all serious and might drop me back a little. I think I know the work but I may easily make slips. At least I always do in my exercises. I expect to be home just for the week end. I wonder could you come over on Sunday? Next week should be my last here. Then I go to Wanstrow for a week and after that (so they say) we have leave to get our kit &c.

De la Mare goes to America on Saturday. I hope he will see Frost.

Maitland wrote that he had none of his kit left that was any use.

Goodbye.

Yours ever

Edward Thomas

The long small room

Trowbridge, November 1916

The long small room that showed willows in the west
Narrowed up to the end the fireplace filled,
Although not wide. I liked it. No one guessed
What need or accident made them so build.

Only the moon, the mouse and the sparrow peeped
In from the ivy round the casement thick.
Of all they saw and heard there they shall keep
The tale for the old ivy and older brick.

When I look back I am like moon, sparrow and mouse
That witnessed what they could never understand
Or alter or prevent in the dark house.
One thing remains the same – this my right hand

Crawling crab-like over the clean white page,
Resting awhile each morning on the pillow,
Then once more starting to crawl on towards age.
The hundred last leaves stream upon the willow.

Letters to Eleanor Farjeon, 15 and 20 November 1916

An earlier draft of the first line of 'The long small room' had
read 'The long small room that showed the distant west'. These
letters record the reasons for Thomas's revision of the line. The
second letter also gives Thomas's response to Farjeon's *Nursery
Rhymes of London Town*.

My dear Eleanor   Wanstrow, Tuesday,
                                         postmarked 15 November 1916

Thank you. It was nice to get a letter out here, where we are billetted
in a big empty house with 2 basins for 42 men. If it rains, I don't know
what will happen. But it is beautiful country that I know a little. We
work from 9 to 4 and then as much as we like. Personally I like to walk
2 hours in the evening. Then we rehearse for the concert, 4 of us are
singing 'Mr McKinley'. Don't come down.

I am worried about the impression the willow made on you. As a

Edward Thomas's Poets

matter of fact I started with that last line as what I was working to. I am only fearing it has a sort of Japanesy suddenness of ending. But it is true, whether or not it is a legitimate switch to make. I will think of it as much like somebody else as possible.

It now seems likely we shall not leave Trowbridge on Saturday in time to come over to you. But later on there will be time, apparently.

Thank you for 'Lights Out', and thank you for your book. I look forward to having it. When I shall read again is quite a serious question, whether I write again or not, and apparently I may. But not here.

Goodbye.

Yours ever

Edward Thomas

My dear Eleanor   Carnforth Station,
                                       postmarked 20 November 1916

Blanco White had some other callers, so I couldn't do what I went there for till about 6.30. It was most tiring. And I never thanked you for the book. But I can now much better because I read every one in the train coming here. I can only say I liked more than half very much and thought practically all the others very good too. It may be that I should have liked all equally if I had not read them straight through – a very absurd test to put them to. I agree that your illustrator is appropriate and never takes the upper hand. If you have any luck you might do well at Christmas.

Well, I did most of my shopping this morning without much enjoying it, as I kept on getting the 2nd best of everything. I shall be back home on Thursday evening and we will suggest some days for you.

By the way if the first line were 'The long small room that showed willows in the west' would it make a difference.

Yours ever

Edward Thomas

The Sheiling

'Travelling back from Gordon Bottomley's
(Silverdale)', 23 November 1916

It stands alone
Up in a land of stone
All worn like ancient stairs,
A land of rocks and trees
Nourished on wind and stone.

And all within
Long delicate has been;
By arts and kindliness
Coloured, sweetened, and warmed
For many years has been.

Safe resting there
Men hear in the travelling air
But music, pictures see
In the same daily land
Painted by the wild air.

One maker's mind
Made both, and the house is kind
To the land that gave it peace,
And the stone has taken the house
To its cold heart and is kind.

Letter to Gordon Bottomley, 30 January 1915

A number of Thomas's letters to Bottomley emphasise the wind
and the rain, as do a number of his poems, such as 'The Source',
'Wind and Mist' and 'The New House'. The description of
Bottomley's house at the end of this letter, although written over
a year earlier than 'The Sheiling', strongly resonates with it.
Thomas's emphasis on weather conditions and physical motion
when composing poetry is reflected in the third verse of 'The
Sheiling', which perhaps also alludes to Bottomley's methods of
composition, as an invalid forced for many years to remain
immobile.

Edward Thomas's Poets

My dear Gordon,   Steep, 30 January 1915

I am sorry to get this news of your mother & all I can hope is that it
will be something that her illness brings you so near to one another.
Incidentally I hope I may see her when I come down to you again.
But it will be strange to see her so when I recall her most plainly
coming towards me over the meadows (which I think you used to call
the Hollow Land: hadn't it a rocky islet or two with beeches on
them?).

We are going to have some changes. It is being arranged that
Mervyn goes over to New Hampshire with the Frosts when they go
next month. He is to join an old schoolmaster friend of ours there for
at any rate 6 months. Perhaps he has seen the last of his schooldays.
He didn't do much good but just kept in the middle of his form. This
may mean we shall leave the neighbourhood of Bedales & seek the
neighbourhood of more real friends than we have there, perhaps the
Ellises in Sussex, which is also much nearer London yet just as far
from its influence. But we haven't begun to talk of this yet. I might
still go to New Hampshire myself if the war ends and leaves things
not too troubled here for me to be free.

Guthrie talks of having to move before very long. I haven't seen
him since he got back from Cornwall. I was laid up 3 weeks with a
sprained ankle & am still a cripple. He has been a good deal relieved
since the war I fancy, & no wonder he feels so easy about his little
pretty schemes. They are so fantastic to me that I can't begin to crit-
icize them as I could if I saw their roots. It would be like saying to a
man Why have you got such a funny face?

You shall have the other Morris when it comes of course, of course.

I keep getting little scraps of work that prevent me from quite seri-
ously facing questions, though I have been interviewing army people
this week to see if there is something like a niche for me to crawl into
excepting a trench. It doesn't look as if there is. My latest job is to be
an English anthology of prose & verse to give as various an impres-
sion as possible of English life, landscape, thought, ambition & glory.
The thing is to arrange it so that it will be as simple & rich as a plum
pudding. Can you suggest any plums or sixpenny bits to be found in
it? I am not going mainly for the explicitly patriotic. It is for the
Oxford Press & is to be done quickly of course. It is to cover the whole
of time from the landing of Brutus to the Zeppelins.

Your house must be like our old one in the wind & rain, but with
the advantage that it is very distinctly divided into an inside & an
outside, whereas ours was like one of those carpets that can be used

either side. So with your cushions & wallpapers & books & gramophone I hope you keep the weather out better.

Is there any news of the new Georgian poetry book, or is it indefinitely postponed? You saw that Hodgson got the *Polignac* £100, I expect. He & I are not meeting till the war is over. I am not patriotic enough for his exuberant taste.

My love to Emily & you.

Yours ever Edward Thomas

Out in the dark

Out in the dark over the snow
The fallow fawns invisible go
With the fallow doe;
And the winds blow
Fast as the stars are slow.

Stealthily the dark haunts round
And, when a lamp goes, without sound
At a swifter bound
Than the swiftest hound,
Arrives, and all else is drowned;

And I and star and wind and deer
Are in the dark together, – near,
Yet far, – and fear
Drums on my ear
In that sage company drear.

How weak and little is the light,
All the universe of sight,
Love and delight,
Before the might,
If you love it not, of night.

Gordon Bottomley, 'In Memoriam Λ.M.W.', 1911, in *Poems and Plays* (London: The Bodley Head, 1953)

Thomas's poem describes visions in the dark; Bottomley's describes voices 'Out of a silence'.

(For a solemn music)

Out of a silence
The voice of music speaks.

When words have no more power,
When tears can tell no more,
The heart of all regret

Is uttered by a falling wave
Of melody.

No more, no more
The voice that gathered us
Shall hush us with deep joy;
But in this hush,
Out of its silence,
In the awaking of music,
It shall return.
For music can renew
Its gladness and communion,
Until we also sink,
Where sinks the voice of music,
Into a silence.

from Robert Frost, 'The Hill Wife', *The Yale Review*, April 1916; *Mountain Interval* (New York: Henry Holt, 1916)

See also Robert Frost's 'The Fear' in *Poetry and Drama*, December 1913 and in *North of Boston*, 1914.

HOUSE FEAR

Always – I tell you this they learned –
Always at night when they returned
To the lonely house from far away
To lamps unlighted and fire gone gray,
They learned to rattle the lock and key
To give whatever might chance to be
Warning and time to be off in flight:
And preferring the out- to the in-door night,
They learned to leave the house-door wide
Until they had lit the lamp inside.

Lascelles Abercrombie, 'Down to the ground like a stone', *Lyrics and Unfinished Poems* (Newtown: The Gregynog Press, 1940)

This poem, written between 1911 and 1914, shares the tight rhymes of 'Out in the dark'.

Down to the ground like a stone
Down from the height
Where the air thins out to nothing but light
Down from the topmost flight
Of life's delight
Lifeless down like a stone
Fell the drone.

John Freeman, 'English Hills', *Stone Trees* (London: Selwyn and Blount, 1916)

On 23 March 1915, Thomas wrote to Freeman about a number of poems (see p. 105). The choice of rhymes in the second verse of 'English Hills' is evocative of 'Out in the dark'.

O that I were
Where breaks the pure cold light
On English hills,
And pewits rising cry,
And gray is all the sky.

Or at evening there
When the faint slow light stays,
And far below
Sleeps the last lingering sound,
And night leans all round.

O then, O there
'Tis English haunted ground.
The diligent stars
Creep out, watch, and smile;
The wise moon lingers awhile.

For surely there
Heroic shapes are moving,
Visible thoughts,
Passions, things divine,
Clear beneath clear star-shine.

O that I were
Again on English hills,

Seeing between
Laborious villages
Her cool dark loveliness.

Letters to Eleanor Farjeon and Myfanwy Thomas, 27 and 29 December 1916

Thomas attributes the origin of 'Out in the dark' to observations made by his daughter Myfanwy. The letter to Myfanwy seems to evoke Frost's 'House Fear' ('The Hill Wife').

My dear Eleanor   R.A. Mess, Tintown, Lydd, 27 December 1916

I only found your cake this morning. It is very good. If you and a cup of tea would appear it would be excellent – only of course I shouldn't mind whether it was or not. I am going to send you in exchange some verses I made on Sunday. It is really Baba who speaks, not I. Something she felt put me on to it. But I am afraid I am meddling now. A real poem would include and imply all these things I am writing, or so I fancy.

I have been both drilling and lecturing today. I am glad they are going to try me as an instructor. But I had to use a greasy door instead of a blackboard.

It is curious how I feel no anxiety or trouble as soon as I am back here, though I was so very glad to be at home.

I will just copy out the verses and send this off. Goodbye. Oh, the Christmas tree was a great success. Baba went pale with surprise as she came into the room and found it. Thank you.

Yours ever
Edward Thomas

My dear Myfanwy,   Tintown, Lydd, 29 December 1916

I am so glad you haven't got that nasty tooth any longer, and I hope you don't dislike the dentist who took it away. But you did enjoy your Christmas, didn't you? I know I did. I mean I enjoyed your Christmas and mine too. When I got here I found two more presents, a pocket writing case from Uncle Oscar and a piece of cake from Eleanor.

Did Mother tell you I wrote a poem about the dark that evening when you did not want to go into the sitting room because it was dark? Eleanor perhaps will type it and then I will send you a copy.

I am going to be very much alone for a few days, because the man who sleeps in my room is going home to Scotland. I think I shall like being alone.

On Monday and Wednesday we are going to shoot with real guns. I don't quite now what I shall have to do. (You see I have spelt 'know' without a k.) But as one of us is away the rest will be uncommonly busy from now onwards. I should not be surprised if we were in France at the end of this month. I do hope peace won't come just yet. I should not know what to do, especially if it came before I had really been a soldier. I wonder if you want peace, and if you can remember when there was no war.

It really is very solitary by this smoky fire with the wind rattling the door, shaking it and making the lock sound as if it were somebody trying to come in but finding the door locked and knowing there was somebody inside who *could* open it.

I think if I had a chair or a table I should write some verses just for something to do before bedtime. Perhaps I will try.

Give Mother and Merfyn and Bronwen each a love for me and tell Mother her letter came this afternoon after I posted my second one to her. Goodbye.

Daddy

Letters on the Poetic Process

Can you single out any poem of which you feel able to tell me the circumstances under which it was written & what relation it bears to 'reality' IF ANY
Edward Thomas to Jesse Berridge, Wick Green,
14 April 1910

Letter to Gordon Bottomley, 22 April 1907

Thomas expresses his disenchantment with Pater's 'external', over-controlled, 'purely self-conscious use of words' and a similar discontent with his own 'forced' critical writings, several years before he wrote *Walter Pater*. He also discusses a review of *The Heart of England* and his approach in writing critical works, showing awareness of how writers can affect each other. The reference to suburban houses relates to ideas for a book on memories of growing up in London suburbs, realised in 1913 as *The Happy-go-lucky Morgans*. There is also evidence of the close relations between Thomas and Davies; Bottomley; A. Martin Freeman, his collaborator on *The Pocket Book*; the writer and editor Ernest Rhys; Roger Ingpen, the future publisher of his *Poems*; Hudson; and de la Mare.

My dear Gordon,   Berryfield Cottage, 22 April 1907

I shall be very glad if you do dedicate a book to me. It is the one thing I should not mind collecting, I think, – dedications: & I shall do well to begin with you and William Davies. I hope the book will not be very long. Will you try Alston Rivers? or is it too long for that shilling series? Davies' *Soul Destroyer* has already appeared in it.

I should not have been so long before writing to you had I not been away a good deal – mainly interviews with a publisher – and then a long visit from Freeman (while Helen & the children were in town): so I got very much behind with my work; and also I have had two bad spells of languor and melancholy. Nor am I likely to be much good just now. For I am trying to give up smoking & apparently my work suffers – as might have been expected – by the sudden drop from 8 pipes a day to 2. It is like me to have started this attempt after Ernest Rhys saying that Swinburne & Dumas both gave up tobacco because it lowered their vitality. Well I know how little vitality I have to lose; yet I thought I might regain a little before it is too late. And I shall want all my energies & more if I am to do my next job well. Probably that will be a life & criticism of Richard Jefferies. It ought to give me many opportunities. There have been two: Besant's excellent advertisement, called a Eulogy and Salt's vigorous but not exhaustive pamphlet. In two years I might do something, knowing the man's native country & his books. Should you hear of any of his early & mostly bad novels – yellow backs – like *The Scarlet Shawl*, I wish you would let me know where. I must have everything here at hand especially as the Museum is closed. It is not quite settled yet, but Hutchinson's reader, Roger Ingpen, thinks I can have £100 in advance of royalties for not over 80,000; & such a book might become a useful property to me – just possibly.

One of my saddest jobs lately has been reviewing John Davidson's drama: *Triumph of Mammon*, with an epilogue. I think his brain must be giving way. There is a lot of energy, as usual; but an unusual incoherence and much less beauty in detail. Of course I couldn't praise it yet I did not like having to say anything against this sad, serious, very 'clever egoist'.

Speaking of reviews, thank you for Scott on me. Frankly, I did not much like it. I wonder does he always write so? or did my book corrupt him? I seem to be able to trace his 'womanly flesh of rivers' – which I think ridiculous – to my 'crystal flesh' which was barely pardonable where I was almost personifying a little river. I cannot think that he really cared for the book & tried to discover what originality it may have: at least it would be hard to learn from it what (if anything) made the book differ from all others or what effect (if any) it produced upon him which no other book could produce. I wonder what you think.

No. Marjoram is a young bank clerk – 22 years old – at Norwich.

Thanks too for Hudson – a trifle & yet with something of his unique personality in it, a personality most dear to me. Rothenstein has just painted him – badly – making him not an eagle in a palace court, but an eagle at the Zoo and contented to be there.

I have made friends with Walter de la Mare. You would like him – a subtle honest person – an accountant in the City (& a clever one, I hear) but rather willing to leave it if he saw a way that would not hurt his wife & 4 children – 34 years old – handsome like young Dickens, but short & his eyes too small – finally he has the foible of liking my reviews & (I fear) preferring them to my landscapes & people who seem to him from a different hand from the *Chronicle* reviewer's, which annoys me.

About Wright's *Pater*. I am told Jackson is a liar & has probably stuffed Wright with lies. If the infatuation is rightly reported, even so it is not sufficiently related to the *Pater* who emerges to justify Wright's treatment of it. I confess I should not be surprised if it were true, but I daresay Pater was physically not equal to his mental pref-

Edward Thomas's Poets

erences. I get more & more dissatisfied with Pater. His work seems fatally external to him – a very wonderful tour de force, but on a level with Greek or Latin verses by a professor. It is often singularly beautiful but even Denys falls short. Pater makes him do things – & how painfully recalcitrant are those bishops kicking the ball in the Cathedral – surely genius would not have allowed us to see the effort (that fails after all) to produce these unusual effects? I wonder do you know what I mean when I say that I do not see the necessity for his work? – I see nothing in it which was beyond his control, no divine agency in it at all. But I need not say that I am suppressing admiration of a great many details & that I believe him to have achieved everything which a purely self-conscious use of words could achieve, more than any other Englishman.

I haven't time to oppose you thoroughly in the subject of my fitness for writing about English poets. It would take too long to explain how forced my criticism nearly always is – how often I *think of things to say* – what a struggle it is to fill a column & how impossible it seems to write at more length. Perhaps my intense desire to say only things that come from the depths & to get on to paper somehow the (perhaps few) passionate moments of my reading life – perhaps this has given a quality to the writing which a friend will not distinguish from perfect sincerity & independence of view.

I don't know Donne very well, but I will. Yes Collins would be better than Gray & of course it was a slip when I forgot Blake.

I am glad of what you say about Suburban houses. I must look at Madox Brown's Work. Is there anything solid and dull about that period of architecture?

Yes, do a play about Gunnar. To give an excuse for hearing those words & seeing that woman on the stage would be true benevolence.

Balmer is in luck & I congratulate him.

Helen says we have room for some of those seedling larkspurs & I should like them.

Goodbye & our love to Emily & you.

Ever yours Edward Thomas

Letter to Edward Garnett, mid-1909

This discussion of the *Light and Twilight* piece 'The Attempt' emphasises Thomas's difficulty in producing the 'simple and direct' language seen in his later poetry.

Dear Garnett,   Ashford, Petersfield, Friday, [mid-1909]

Thank you for your criticisms. I seem to see your meaning in nearly every case and I have altered most of the queried passages and have added a piece which makes the whole more intelligible. You will see that from the start his chances of pulling the trigger were small. Perhaps he is even more morbid and self conscious than you thought, and thus perhaps the last part of p. 4 will no longer seem 'intolerably affected', especially as these considerations do not – as I point out – really weigh with him in his decision. You are unjust in your view of what you call literary 'phrases that smell of the lamp'. Such phrases however bad come to me without thinking or seeking. It is your 'simple and direct' phrases that I have to seek for. I think you might accept my objectionable gracefulness now as no office of mine. – About the first pages I cannot decide, but was inclined to think they should stand as they – and even their 'leisureliness' – help to suggest the man who is going to make a fool of himself once more.

If you approve I should be glad if you would offer it to 'Country Life'. I am writing nothing but stories and sketches and episodes now. Thank you again.

Yours ever
Edward Thomas

Letter to Walter de la Mare, 7 September 1913

Thomas records an early attempt at poetry, over a year before he started writing his mature poems. This attempt is also described in his essay 'Insomnia' in *The Last Sheaf*. As in the letter, the essay stresses his situation, sleepless, with nothing to do, and links his failure to finish the poem to his compulsion, 'trying hard', to complete it, and to the tyranny of rhyme.

My dear de la Mare,   Selsfield House [7 September 1913]

I am sorry about today. Ellis couldn't come because his wife's bicycle was useless & we couldn't hire one. Well, I started before 3, got a puncture in a mile, mended it, but in getting the tyre back ripped the tube, returned here & mended that, started again after 4 & found my tyre flat at the point I had reached before. So I could not come & was sick with, & soon afterwards sick of, myself. I am very sorry to have had you expecting me vainly. However, I have written to my wife about next Sunday & we will let you know as soon as we can what can be done. I hope your wife has got over the packing & the return without too much trouble.

This address will most likely find me till Saturday morning, tho it is not the time & place to do nothing in, which is all I have to do, except that in sleepless hours this morning I found myself (for the first time) trying hard to *rhyme* my mood & failing very badly indeed, in fact comically so, as I could not complete the first verse or get beyond the rhyme of ember & September. This must explain any future lenience towards the mob of gentlemen that rhyme with ease.

Yours ever
Edward Thomas

Letter to John Freeman, December 1913

This letter describes Thomas's experiments in achieving sponteneity in writing. This approach chimes with his later declarations, to Frost and Freeman in May and June 1915, of the importance of simultaneity of conception and execution in poetic composition, and contrasts with his earlier Paterian 'self conscious' use of words. With the image of the wall of China, Thomas not only suggests a huge impasse but indicates ways of getting beyond it.

My dear Freeman,   Selsfield House, East Grinstead,
                                     [December 1913]

I send the book. It is best begun at the end, I believe. I wish I could come on Monday evening but it is my only one and I can't. It is just possible I may be free at lunch on Tuesday: if so I will let you know.

The difficulty about the autobiography is arrangement. There are a few landmarks & I can place most details within a year or two between; but at present I am letting one flow out of another in a manner which may ultimately mean chaos or a child's garden of prose altogether run wild. What I fear is that it will be a disjointed series of short passages like all my books. I put down almost every trifle because if it turns out well nothing will be trifling. Up to 12 years old it is practically all being doing & suffering, no thoughts or sensations. I (at 35) interfere as little as possible. 11–14 was a deadly material period with no poetry read or acted & I am at it now. When you say you don't remember anything till 10 or 12 I expect you ignore all the disintegrated fragments I have put down by the score – books, people, places. I had no religious sense, only a dull fretful hate of religious exteriors. I don't pretend to say everything. But after all, the book is mainly an occupation for the days when I've no work & I have nothing to be at but vain thought that comes against a wall of China every 5 minutes & I can't fly nor have the patience to mine.

I shall be sorry if we cannot meet.

Yours ever

Edward Thomas

Letter to Robert Frost, 19 May 1914

In May 1914, Thomas published two articles in *T.P.'s Weekly*, on Hudson, and on the cuckoo.

My dear Frost,   Steep, 19 May 1914

I wish I could write a letter. But everyday I write a short Welsh sketch & a review. I read a bit & weed a bit & every evening type something, not to speak of touching the fiction still sporadically. And then there is the weather to enjoy or (here comes the laugh) to imagine how it should be enjoyed. Today I was out from 12 till sunset bicycling to the pine country by Ascot & back. But it all fleets & one cannot lock up at evening the cake one ate during the day. There must be a world where that is done. I hope you & I will meet in it. I hardly expect it of New Hampshire more than of old. – I was glad Hudson turned out as I hoped he would. I understand those 3 approaches. If only you were to be in town & he too & he well & not afflicted by his sick wife & age coming on I would take you to see him. He is, if anything, more than his books. Don't get at me about my T.P. article, which wasn't all that even I could do, but a series of extracts from an essay I shan't do. You could do one now. And you really should start doing a book on speech and literature, or you will find me mistaking your ideas for mine & doing it myself. You can't prevent me from making use of them: I do so daily & want to begin over again with them & wring all the necks of my rhetoric – the geese. However, my 'Pater' would show you I had got onto the scent already.

Your second note pleased me. I shall perhaps come soon. My wife & I are to have a week or so very probably in early July. We *have* to fit in several calls. If we can we will come to Ledington. I assume there would be room (for 2 whole days).

Did Davies appear? He had left town when I was there last. – I go up next about June 5.

Bronwen is suffering from flat feet & a stoop. She enjoys the new school & the gymnastics. But we miss her. She won't be home till August. Now about August, could we *all* get into the Chandler's for a month & would they have us & at what price? The only difficulty would be a room for me to work in. For work I must. Will you consider? We shall try to let this cottage.

I don't hear when your book is coming. I tried to get T.P. to let me write on it but they won't.

I wonder whether you can imagine me taking to verse. If you can I might get over the feeling that it is impossible – which at once obliges your good nature to say 'I can'. In any case I must have my 'writer's melancholy' though I can quite agree with you that I might spare some of it to the deficient. On the other hand even with registered post, telegraph &c & all modern conveniences I doubt if I can transmit it.

I am pleased with myself for hitting on 'Mowing' & 'The Tuft of Flowers'. For I forgot the names of those you meant me particularly to read, these I suppose being amongst them. You see that conceit consorts with writer's melancholy. I go on writing something every day. Sometimes brief unrestrained impressions of things lately seen, like a drover with 6 newly shorn sheep in a line across a cool woody road on market morning & me looking back to envy him & him looking back at me for some reason which I cannot speculate on. Is this North of Bostonism?

Goodbye & I hope you are all well. Mervyn has been writing to Lesley I see. I hope he will go North of Boston before it is too late – North of Boston & west of me.

Yours ever
Edward Thomas

Letter to John Freeman, 8 March 1915

Thomas writes on his admiration for birdsong; the relation between his prose and his poetry; the influence of Frost; and, in his criticism of Abercrombie, his growing preference for what is not forced, self-conscious or made up.

My dear Freeman,   Coventry, 8 March 1915

The 20th then and early. I believe the 8.55 still runs and another something before 11 (getting in at 1.15) but make sure about this just before the day as there are so many changes nowadays. If I could produce a nightingale on March 20 do you think I should bother about being a bard? I wish I could. Now if it were a very very pretty March 20 the Lord might produce a chiffchaff but since I hurt my ankle I have seen nothing & it isn't a real ankle yet by a long way.

The Anthology is substantially done. It grows slowly now while I am waiting for the Oxford Press reader's judgement. (He is J.C. Smith, who edited Spenser's *Fairie Queene*.) All that typing & turning over pages knocked all the rapture about as far off as the nearest nightingales. Then came a beastly index & a beastly book on Babylon (to review). Now I've had more at the Museum & still have a day of it left. Then I hope to put myself in an attitude worthy of the Muse's indulgence more. Whether the habit of writing will make me command it more often than I deserve it, & whether that will be quite fatal to success, *I* can't say. My pseudonym is just a family name, Edward Eastaway. I never thought of Gibson. It would have been a lark. So far I have heard no news. By the way what I have done so far have been like quintessences of the best parts of my prose books – not much sharper or more intense, but I hope a little & since the first take off they haven't been Frosty very much, or so I imagine & I have tried as often as possible to avoid the facilities offered by blank verse. I try not to be long – I even have an ambition to keep under 12 lines (but rarely succeed).

I've not dipped into New Numbers yet. Drinkwater is hopeless. Gibson, for me, almost equally so. Abercrombie, I fancy, applies the lash, & I wonder whether he always did. I used to think he was naturally a spirited steed. I am always anxious to like him.

We haven't heard yet from Mervyn. His ship arrived 12 days ago so we might do soon.

By the way I got Doughty for my Anthology. He was very nice.

Yours ever

E.T.

Letter to Jesse Berridge, 1 June 1915

> This letter is significant for its instruction on how to read Thomas's poems by considering their 'unfinish'. The engagement in Gloucester was with J.W. Haines, when Thomas was composing 'I built myself a house of glass' and 'Words'.

My dear Jesse,   Steep, Petersfield, 1 June 1915

I am very glad to get your news. Of course my verses would not be good reading for you if you are reading the papers a lot. There's the difference. I can't read them. I wait for them & then when they come I am through them in five minutes standing up ready to go up the hill & do a great slab of Marlborough. Well I think I can end it in 3 full weeks & so be free for you. 1 ride would clear my head best I think, if it suits you. We could go to Avebury & up round. I don't know how many days you will spare. But I have an engagement in Gloucester about that time & we might end up there. You could come here for a night, or else we could meet at Reading say. Of course I can't swear I shall be done, but I really think so if things go on as they do. Stuart Reid's book was no good.

I am so glad you like your garden & hope you have really got your ears back again now. And it is good news that Dell gets on & enjoys it. I hope he will do well. Give him my love.

Send the verses back when you have done with them. I fancy they are sufficiently new in their way to be unacceptable if the reader gets caught up by their way & doesn't get any effect before he begins to consider & see their 'unfinish'.

Yours ever with our love to you all
Edward Thomas

Letter to J.W. Haines, 15 August 1915

The criticism of Haines's poems is revealing about Thomas's poetic processes.

My dear Haines,   Steep, Petersfield, 15 August 1915

I don't know if one has the right to be plain unless one is sure one doesn't mind others using the right. But I shall be plain and say that reading your poems makes me feel that you do not express yourself in verse. As it seems to me rhyme and metre compel you to paraphrase what you would have said or sometimes not said at all, had you not formed the habit; and after it all, what you individually feel or think remains unexpressed, at most faintly suggested to a sympathetic reader, if I may dare to call myself one on top of this. The subject is endless. You can't judge yourself. You know your intentions. You know the experiences out of which your poems spring. You can't separate the poems from those intentions and experiences. I don't know how many of us can. I don't pretend to be able to myself, but I do feel sure that I am right in your case, though I may not have put it plainly. I might be plainer at greater length and to no purpose. I can't expect to convince you. I don't know why I should want to

convince you. In fact, as I hinted at first, I doubt whether I have the
right to say what I have said, and I ask to be forgiven if I seem to
intrude as a reviewer into private life. For I know how I should feel if
I got this letter myself. But I could not lie out and out. It would have
been even more unpleasant to beat about the bush and leave you to
guess at my meaning than it is to speak like this. I can't imagine if it
would have been more unpleasant to you. I would lie to an idiot. I
would beat about the bush to an old fool. There are other categories
where I should feel powerless to say what I thought, but I must not
attempt to dictate to you how you should treat my plainness.

Yours ever

E. Thomas

Letter to Robert Frost, 15 August 1916

In this letter Thomas explains how boredom can act to enforce
concentration. He also alludes to 'Fifty Faggots' and reveals a
deliberately cultivated preference for verbs over adjectives.

My dear Robert,   13 Rusham Rd, Balham, London SW,
                                          15 August 1916

This will be our best address in future. We are leaving from Steep to
give Mervyn a home near his work, & we have not yet decided on the
new cottage. It may be at High Beech, a few yards from my first camp.
I have had you all in mind continually these last few days. For I have
been at Steep on sick leave after vaccination, which gave me
headaches &c for a week. Much of the time I spent in sorting letters,
papers & books, as I may not have a home for some time to come.
Helen & the children are going to the seaside. I may go at any moment
to my new unit which may be in London & may be anywhere. They
will move during September & soon after that I might be far off. This
waiting troubles me. I really want to be out. However, I daresay I
shan't be till the winter. I wrote some lines after a period in hospital
– largely because to concentrate is the only happy thing possible when
one is bored & helpless. Today came a chance of getting a book out.
A brother in law of De la Mare's publishes in a small way & I am to
send him a batch to look at. De la Mare talks of going out to America
in October. I hope you will see him at last.

No news of Haines since he joined.

Eleanor Farjeon is roaming around in the fine weather. Somebody
said today that one realised the blessing of peace & leisure now. I

contradicted him. I don't believe I often had as good times as I have had, one way & another, these past 13 months. My faggot pile is pretty nearly used up, but it wasn't fair. We have been saving coal by wood fires out of doors, or it would have lasted the war out I believe.

I want to see your handwriting again soon, though I have seen so much of it these past few days with the address Ledington, Ryton, Beaconsfield.

I brought a big load of books up with me to sell today & am sending away 2 more cases. I burnt a pile that would have roasted a sheep 2 nights ago.

No news of anyone. Hudson is still an invalid, I fear. Garnett is away. I have not seen him for 14 months. Bottomley I may see at the end of the month when everyone is away & I may have some leave between leaving my old corps & joining the new. I should like to go up there and bathe in the lake with the bird's eye primroses & the silver sand. There is nothing like the solitude of a solitary lake in early morning, when one is in deep still water. More adjectives here than I allow myself now & fewer verbs.

Goodbye all & my love to you all.

Ever yours

Edward Thomas

Letter to J.W. Haines, 15 September 1916

This letter contains specific comments on a number of Thomas's poems.

My dear Haines,

13 Rusham Rd, Balham, London SW,

15 September 1916

I may go to Trowbridge on Friday. Then perhaps I get over to you. From all I hear about the barracks there I shall be glad to escape, but I don't know yet what the leave amounts to. I will write again. Up to now I have been so unwell with a cold following on a very rundown condition after vaccination that I have made no use of my weekends.

I like reading over your comments on my verses. 'Roads' I think one of the best. 'Helen of the roads' is simply a Welsh goddess who is connected with roads. Many of the Roman roads in Wales are called Sarn Helen or Helen's Causeway. She comes in the Dream of Maxen in the Mabinogion. Then I like 'The Unknown' & refuse to believe it is clever, tho' I admit it is a bit quicker than the rest. 'After you speak' I believe is all right and 'The Weasel'. Nobody has cared much for 'The Ash Grove'. 'How at once should I know' is perhaps natural history. The poems to the children I hope are among the best. I wonder how they will look in a book. There is a chance of their appearing before very long. Also a fair selection is to appear in Trevelyan's 'Annual' (Constable).

Wilfrid Childe I seem to remember in the Oxford Poems of 1910–1912, or whatever it was. But I don't remember his books at all. I don't see any books new or old now.

I shall be glad to get out of London though I can see friends there. I am going down to Steep now with my wife – the first bit of the country I have seen it will be since I left Romford a month ago.

The new work is difficult, especially as I am unfit and the instructors are bad. We have 7 weeks more at Trowbridge and then may be gazetted. I want to go out badly now.

I heard from Frost at last. He has been reading publically for a fund in aid of the wounded in France. He has been writing but did not send anything. He said nothing about his family. Carol has been ill I know. It was a more cheerful letter than I have had.

My love to you all three,

Yours ever

Edward Thomas

Edward Thomas's Literary Friends and Correspondents

Lascelles Abercrombie (1881–1938)
Thomas and the poet and literary critic Lascelles Abercrombie reviewed each other's work. In the *Daily Chronicle* for 29 February 1908, Thomas wrote of Abercrombie's *Interludes and Poems*, 'there is only one English dramatist who has gone beyond this poet in making blank verse, the march or leap or stagger or crawl or hesitation of the syllables correspond to varying emotions with thrilling delicacy.' Later, he was more critical, observing in the 28 December 1911 *Daily Chronicle* that Abercrombie's *Emblems of Love* 'is all glittering, crashing, hurrying abundance, endless multiplication, disorder, and sputtering violence.' Thomas first met Abercrombie in April 1914 in Dymock, Gloucestershire. They planned to go walking in Wales but the war intervened.

Jesse Berridge (1874–1966)
After working as a bank clerk, Jesse Berridge trained as an Anglican priest in 1905. He and Thomas first met in 1901. At this time, they both had young families and were living frugally in West London. They tended to meet about once a year, going on trips to the country, and sustained a sparse but regular correspondence. Berridge published two books of poems in 1902. Thomas did not rate these highly, and found Berridge's response to his own verse lacking. In 1914 they discussed collaborating on a novel. In 1915, Thomas wrote to Frost that Berridge 'tries awfully hard to like my verses – his ideal, when he was literary, being Plato-Rossetti', but also said that Berridge was 'the saintliest, honestest, best-natured man imaginable, doesn't like everybody but thinks ill of nobody'. Thomas was close to Berridge's eldest son Dell and in 1912 dedicated his book of retold legends, *Norse Tales*, to the Berridge family.

Gordon Bottomley (1874–1948)

The poet and verse dramatist Gordon Bottomley was often confined to bed with illness. He first wrote to Thomas in 1902, although James Ashcroft Noble, Thomas's first mentor and future father-in-law, had shown Thomas some of Bottomley's verses seven years earlier. They shared an interest in literature, folk song, ancient myths and legends. Thomas dedicated *Rose Acre Papers* to Bottomley. Bottomley's wife Emily occasionally acted as scribe when Bottomley was too ill to write. The letters provide a record of their intimate friendship, their habit of mutual criticism and close collaboration, and Thomas's respect for Bottomley's early creative work, as well as his later questioning of what he perceived as 'made up' methods of composition. Thomas visited Bottomley several times in the Lake District and celebrates these times in his poem 'The Sheiling'. Bottomley organised the publication of some of Thomas's poems in Abercrombie and R.C. Trevelyan's *An Annual of New Poetry* in 1917.

W.H. Davies (1871–1940)

William Henry Davies, a Welsh poet and writer, is the author of *The Autobiography of a Super-Tramp* written in 1908, an account of his times in the United States between 1893 and 1899. On his return to England in 1905 he published *The Soul's Destroyer*, which Thomas reviewed under the title 'A POET AT LAST!', writing to Berridge on 16 October 1905 that it was 'full of things that nobody else could have written in 20 years'. In a letter to Bottomley written on 26 December 1906 he praised Davies for his ability to 'attain simplicity unawares'. Davies's work bore resemblances to *The Pocket Book of Poems and Songs for the Open Air*, the anthology of ballads and songs that Thomas was compiling at this time. Although not well off, Thomas helped subsidise Davies, inviting him to share his small study cottage and enlisting the help of others. Davies spent many evenings with Thomas's family and dedicated *New Poems* (1907) to Thomas and his wife. Thomas persuaded George Bernard Shaw to write an introduction to *The Autobiography of a Super-Tramp* and advised Davies on his manuscript poems.

Walter de la Mare (1873–1956)

Walter de la Mare, the poet, short story writer and novelist, worked in the statistics department of the London office of Standard Oil for eighteen years. In 1908, he received a Civil List pension and concentrated on his writing. He worked as a literary reviewer for the *Bookman* and from 1911 became the chief reviewer for the *Times*

Literary Supplement. In 1906, de la Mare wrote to Thomas to express appreciation of Thomas's reviews of his work. They quickly became friends, Thomas describing de la Mare to Bottomley in 1907 as 'a subtle honest person', and referring on 19 July 1909 to 'his singularly (sometimes comically) restless & curious & innocent mind'. They met regularly at each other's houses and at least at one point worked together at one of Thomas's writing retreats, Dillybrook Farm in Wiltshire. The de la Mares rented a cottage near the Thomases in Steep each summer, and the two families' children frequently exchanged visits. Thomas and de la Mare reviewed each other in the press, gave each other criticism and advice on each other's writings and publishing opportunities and de la Mare shared his London Library borrowing privileges with Thomas. In 1912 Thomas dedicated *Swinburne* to de la Mare. He esteemed de la Mare's work very highly, describing his poetry collection *Peacock Pie* as comparable only to Frost's *North of Boston*. Thomas's later letters reflect a growing distrust, possibly due to de la Mare's public success and comparative wealth, and to Thomas's growing intimacy with Frost which tended to eclipse other close writing friendships.

Eleanor Farjeon (1881–1965)
Eleanor Farjeon was a poet and writer of children's stories. She first met Thomas in late 1912, when she was a shy and impressionable 31-year-old. They soon became very close, and her friendship with him extended to his wife and children with whom she also spent much time. Thomas's frequent letters to her refer to his depressive moods, and the doings and sayings of his children. Once he started writing poems, she acted as a willing typist of successive poetic drafts, commenting in detail on them, particularly their use of rhythm and rhyme. Thomas dedicated his book of retold proverbs *Four-and-Twenty Blackbirds* to her and the writer and editor Clifford Bax in 1915. This book has similarities with her own *Nursery Rhymes of London Town* (1916), but was composed at least a year earlier. Thomas's comments on her story 'The Soul of Kol Nikon' in 1913 were not favourable, but he responded more positively to what he called her 'London Rhymes'.

John Freeman (1880–1929)
John Freeman was a poet and essayist, working in insurance in London. De la Mare, a close friend of Freeman's, sent Thomas some of Freeman's poems for comment at the end of 1907. Thomas observed that the poems showed 'he could write & had a special

individual feeling for words'. A direct correspondence between Freeman and Thomas began in January 1909, after Freeman sent Thomas his *Twenty Poems*. They discussed books and each other's work in progress. In time, Thomas's opinion of Freeman's work became less enthusiastic, and he observed to Bottomley in May 1916 that 'John Freeman's [poems] weren't a bit in my line, but the angel (he is one) didn't mind my not concealing it.' Thomas's youngest daughter frequently went to stay with the Freemans, who had a young daughter of their own, and his 1914 letters to Freeman, when Thomas was embarking on his mature poetry, reveal an acute awareness of his daughter's perceptions and early experimentations with language.

Robert Frost (1874–1963)
Robert Frost came to England from America in 1912. His *A Boy's Will* was published the next year. His next book, *North of Boston*, was enthusiastically reviewed by Thomas in 1914 as 'one of the most revolutionary books of modern times'. Thomas and Frost first met in late 1913 and soon became close friends. Their children also became close and worked together on a literary magazine *The Bouquet*, to which Thomas and Frost contributed. In the summer of 1914 Thomas and his family spent a month with Frost's family in Dymock, Gloucestershire, where the two discussed poems and theories of poetry, in particular the relation of poetry to speech rhythms. Thomas's poem 'The sun used to shine' celebrates this time. Thomas acknowledged Frost as the 'only begetter' of his mature poetry, and dedicated his *Poems* (1917) to him. Frost returned to America in 1915 and bought a farm in New Hampshire, urging Thomas to join him. Thomas enlisted instead, but they continued to correspond and send each other their poems. Thomas wrote in October 1915 that 'the next best thing to having you here is having the space (not a void) that nobody else can fill'. He talked of joining Frost in America after the war.

Edward Garnett (1868–1937)
Edward Garnett was a writer, critic and literary editor. He was the reader for Duckworth when Thomas sent them *Horae Solitariae* in 1902. His literary contacts and correspondents were extensive, and from 1905 he began to hold weekly lunches in Soho, which Thomas regularly attended. Thomas became very friendly both with Garnett and his son David. Garnett commented on much of Thomas's work, including his poems, as well as encouraging him socially and giving

him advice on his career. Thomas did not respect Garnett as a creative writer, calling his *An Imaged World: Poems in Prose* (1894) 'stupid, without power & without effort' in a letter to Bottomley (3 May 1905). Curiously, however, the prose poem in that work, 'Spring in a London Square', bears a number of similarities to Thomas's 'A Group of Statuary' in *Light and Twilight* (1911). Thomas initially valued Garnett's critical opinion highly, calling him a 'damnably infallible' critic in a letter of 15 Setember 1905 to Gordon Bottomley. However, after he had begun to write his mature poetry he expressed disagreement with Garnett's criticism on more than one occasion.

J.W. Haines (1875–1960)
Jack Haines, a solicitor and amateur botanist living in Gloucester, met Thomas through Frost in the autumn of 1914. Thomas often stayed with him. Haines, unusually among Thomas's correspondents, guessed that Thomas was the author of the 'Edward Eastaway' poems in *This England*. Haines records how Frost used to read to him both his own poems and Thomas's *Four-and-Twenty Blackbirds*. Haines also wrote poems, which Thomas disliked, writing to Frost on 28 June 1915 that 'he is a good soul, & he only read one of his poems, a thing about a number of different flowers in the Lake District, incredibly undistinguished. I doubt if a botanist can write tolerably about flowers.'

W.H. Hudson (1841–1922)
The author, naturalist and ornithologist William Henry Hudson was born of American parents in Argentina and settled in England in 1869. He produced a series of ornithological studies. He wrote many books on the English countryside, including *Hampshire Days* (1903), *Afoot in England* (1909) and *A Shepherd's Life* (1910). He also wrote the novel *Green Mansions* (1904). In a letter to Eleanor Farjeon, Thomas called Hudson's *Adventures Among Birds* (1913), 'about the best bird book there is'. He came to know Hudson through Garnett in 1906, and became very fond of Hudson both as a man and a writer, dedicating *Richard Jefferies* to him. He wrote of Hudson to Bottomley on 26 February 1908: 'Except William Morris there is no other man whom I would sometimes like to have been, no other writing man.' Hudson was very perceptive about Thomas, writing to Garnett on 29 December 1913, after reading Thomas's novel *The Happy-go-lucky Morgans*, that 'he has taken the wrong path and is wandering lost in the vast wilderness' and 'is essentially a poet'. However, he did

not rate Thomas's poetry highly, writing to Morley Roberts after Thomas's death in 1917 that 'I had a thin volume of verses by Edward Thomas sent me a few days ago but find his poetic gift was a rather small one.'

Notes

1914

'**November Sky**': The letter to Frost refers to Edward Marsh (E.M.), editor of the five *Georgian Poetry* anthologies between 1912 and 1922, and Harold Monro, proprietor of the Poetry Bookshop and closely involved with the Georgian poetry anthologies. Frost and his family were staying at the poet Lascelles Abercrombie's house in Ryton. There are echoes of Thomas's 'November Sky' in John Freeman's 'November Skies', published in *Stone Trees* (1916), but possibly written much earlier.

'**After Rain**': In January 1915 Thomas sprained his ankle and was laid up for a number of weeks, during which time he composed several poems, including 'After Rain'. The 10 and 16 January letters to Eleanor Farjeon comprise some of their discussions on rhyme. In *Edward Thomas: The Last Four Years* (1958), Eleanor Farjeon describes the songs of Stanley North, a mercurial artist in stained glass, as 'ribald' (p. 110). The party mentioned in the second letter was for the medical doctor Maitland Radford. Viola Meynell was a novelist and poet.

'**Interval**': This poem is also discussed in a letter to Eleanor Farjeon of 10 January 1915 (pp. 8–9). The 'monkey's tale' in the de la Mare letter refers to his children's book *The Three Mulla-Mulgars*. See also de la Mare's 'Snow' (p. 21).

'**The Mountain Chapel**': See Thomas's 'The Pond'. Thomas's 'Birds in March' in *Young Days* (Sunday School Association journal, February 1895) includes the passage: '[A] woodland mere, and amidst the reeds and rushes growing along the shore, or in the shallow water at the edge, we spy a moor-hen's nest approaching completion. It is made of the long bayonet-like reeds and other water plants.'

'**The Manor Farm**': In the 13 March 1915 letter to Garnett, Thomas refers to Shelley's 'The Sensitive Plant'. Thomas retitled 'May 20' as 'May 23' in his letter to Hudson of 23 March 1915. Garnett held weekly literary lunches at Mt Blanc, a Soho restaurant. The offices of the publisher Duckworth's were at 3 Henrietta St.

1915

'**The Source**': 'Niflheim' in the letter to Bottomley is the underworld in Norse mythology. Swansea's defeat was in rugby. The 'rain & wind' comments in the letter to Frost of 15 May 1915 (p. 59) may also refer to 'The Source'.

'**Snow**': De la Mare refers to Thomas's 'Snow' in his 2 January 1919 *Times Literary Supplement* review of Thomas's *Last Poems*. In the letter to de la Mare, 'Ecstasy' refers to a monograph Thomas was attempting to write for Batsford. 'W.H.' refers to the publishers W.H. Heinemann. De la Mare lived at Cowden and Thomas also met him at Anerly. In the letter to Eleanor Farjeon 'L'Isolée' and 'The Cragsman' are poems in Geoffrey Winthrop Young's *Freedom: Poems* (1914).

'**The Lofty Sky**': In the letter to Berridge, Dell is Berridge's eldest son; Edna is his wife; the job is a chaplaincy and the article is Thomas's 'This England', published in *The English Review*, April 1915.

'**The Child on the Cliff**': Mervyn's 'detention' in the letter to Eleanor Farjeon refers to the experience of Thomas's son. Accompanying the Frosts to America, he was briefly detained on entry to the States. Thomas sent out poems under a pseudonym from Eleanor Farjeon's address. 'Stanley' is probably Stanley North, a stained glass artist (see Note to 'After Rain', p. 189 above).

'**But these things also**': In the letter to Garnett 'Hueffer' is Ford (Hueffer) Madox Ford. Thomas refers to reviews of Frost's *North of Boston*, and also to Frost's *A Boy's Will*.

'**The New House**': The letter to Bottomley refers to the poet and antique-dealer Vivian Locke Ellis, who lived at Selsfield House, East Grinstead, where Thomas often stayed as a paying guest when writing his books.

'**Two Pewits**': In the letter to Garnett, 'Dials' & 'Poetry' refer to American literary magazines. Garnett wrote an article on Frost for the August 1915 *Atlantic Monthly*. The discussion of 'because' is a reference to line 16 of 'Lob'. Thomas researched *The Duke of Marlborough* at the British Museum. The 'proverb stories' are '*Four-and-Twenty Blackbirds*. The letter to Eleanor Farjeon refers to Harold Monro, proprietor of the Poetry Bookshop, and the writer, critic and editor Clifford Bax.

'**Wind and Mist**': The letter to Bottomley of 11 November 1906 refers to Thomas's country book *The Heart of England*; his anthology *The Pocket Book of Songs and Poems for the Open Air*; 'Goatfoot' or 'The Dairy-maids to Pan', a lyric by Bottomley; and Thomas's Welsh 'translation', 'Eluned', in *Beautiful Wales*. (For the text of 'Eluned', see pp. 67–8.) The 26 August 1910 letter refers to Thomas's book on inspiration, *Feminine Influence on the Poets*. 'July' appeared in *Light and Twilight* in 1911. He also refers to Joseph Conrad and Ford (Hueffer) Madox Ford.

'**Lob**': In the first few months of 1915, Thomas was compiling his anthology *This England*. As Edna Longley writes in *Poems and Last Poems*, this anthology acts as 'a source-book' for 'Lob'. One contemporary source is

Thomas Hardy's 'blackbird's "pret-ty de-urr!"' in 'The Spring Call' (*Time's Laughingstocks*, 1909). Thomas reviewed this book in the 7 December 1909 *Daily Chronicle* and the 9 December 1909 *Morning Post*, and anthologised 'The Spring Call' in *This England*. Another contemporary source is T. Sturge Moore's 'The lubber, while rats thieve, / Laughs in his sleeve' from 'Lubber Breeze' (*The Little School: A Posy of Poems*, 1905). Thomas anthologised 'Lubber Breeze' in *The Pocket Book* and quoted it in a 2 September 1905 *Academy* review, writing that the poem was 'as engrossing as an ant's nest, an old doll, a swan's feather, [...] we see the child in some of the rhythms; they dance'. In the letter to Freeman, Joy is Freeman's daughter; the comment on the treaty probably refers to the Treaty of London of 1839 which guaranteed Belgian neutrality and provided the rationale for Britain's decision to go to war in 1914.

'**Digging [1]**' See also the last two lines of Davies's 'The Owl' (p. 28).

'**Home [2]**': There are similarities between 'Home [2]' and Hardy's 'The Darkling Thrush' in *Poems of the Past and Present* (1901), a poem that Thomas anthologised in *The Pocket Book*. Hardy refers to the 'full-hearted evensong' of a thrush and 'Some blessed Hope, whereof he knew/ And I was unaware.' 'Men know but little more than we' is the first line of Hardy's 'The Caged Thrush Freed and Home Again' (*Poems of the Past and Present*, 1901). 'Home [2]' also appears to echo Michael Fairless [Margaret Fairless Barber]'s *The Roadmender* (1902), which includes the words, 'So I sat, hammering out my thoughts, and with them the conviction that stonebreaking should be allotted to minor poets of vagrant children of nature like myself.' Thomas described *The Roadmender* in a 12 March 1902 letter to Berridge as 'exquisite minor prose', reviewing it in the 23 and 25 March 1902 *Daily Chronicle*, and grouping it, in a letter to Bottomley on 10 November 1902, with passages in Keats and Yeats that 'quite overcome my intelligence' (p. 47). The 5 November 1913 letter to Eleanor Farjeon is written from Ellis's house, where Thomas was writing *Keats*. He refers to the writer and editor Clifford Bax and to Godwin Baynes, a nervous disorder specialist who treated Thomas, and later became the champion of Jung.

'**April**' The letter to Frost mentions the literary editor R.A. Scott-James and Bronwen, Thomas's elder daughter.

'**Fifty Faggots**': The British liner *Lusitania* mentioned in the 15 May 1915 letter to Frost was torpedoed on 7 May 1915. The poet Ralph Hodgson was a close friend of Thomas's. Thomas's reservations about Rupert Brooke's work, as implied in the 9 September 1916 letter to Frost, are discussed more fully in a 3 May 1915 letter (p. 55). 'The Old Cloak' was the title of an anthology of 'the homely' that Thomas and Frost intended to work on after the war.

'**I built myself a house of glass**': In the letter to Eleanor Farjeon, 'the Old Balaban' refers to a typist's two-piece support for a manuscript. The reference to glass houses could allude to Thomas's *Four-and-Twenty*

Blackbirds story 'People who Live in Glass Houses shouldn't throw Stones', or to Farjeon's poem 'Glasshouse Street', written by 1915 and published in *Nursery Rhymes of London Town* (1916). Garnett notes in his introduction to *Selected Poems of Edward Thomas* that: 'The poignant lines 'I Built Myself a House of Glass' (which he [Thomas] wrote in a letter to me by way of self-exculpation) have a sad certainty.' The 'Civil List' in the Garnett letter refers to an application for a grant for Thomas. Garnett served abroad as a civilian nursing orderly from July to December 1915. David is Garnett's son.

'**Words**': In a 15 December 1914 letter to Haines Thomas writes of Geoffrey Winthrop Young's *Freedom* poems: 'Rather few are really good, but those are good, and it is all interesting.' Young's 'Pixy Pool' (in *Freedom*, 1914), also bears some similarity to lines in Thomas's 'Over The Hills'. Another poem that resonates with 'Words' is John Freeman's 'English Hills' (p. 165). For a letter from Thomas to Freeman of 23 March 1915 referring to a number of Freeman's poems later published in *Stone Trees*, see pp. 105–6.

'**Haymaking**': The origin of the bow and arrow conceit in 'Haymaking' has been attributed to a poem by Frost's daughter Lesley, 'What A Swallow Must Be' in *The Bouquet*, July 1914. Thomas also uses the image in 'The Swifts', and in 'The Artist' (*Light and Twilight*, 1911). Similar uses of the image occur in Richard Jefferies's *The Amateur Poacher* (1870), and Thomas Hardy's 'On Sturminster Foot-Bridge'.

'**Aspens**': Frost wrote to Thomas on 31 July 1915 that 'Aspens' 'seems the loveliest of all'. See Thomas Hardy's 'The Pine Planters' (*Cornhill Magazine*, June 1903), and *Time's Laughingstocks* (1909).

'**Digging [2]**': In the 21 July 1915 letter to Eleanor Farjeon, 'prophet' alludes to Thomas's expectation that his verses would cease with enlisting. Canon Hardwicke Rawnsley, 1851–1920, a founder of the National Trust, was a prolific sonnet writer.

'**Cock-Crow**': See also A.E. Housman's 'Wake: the silver dusk returning' and 'Up, lad, up, 'tis late for lying' in 'Reveille', *A Shropshire Lad* (1896), anthologised as the opening poem in Thomas's *The Pocket Book*. The letter to Bottomley refers to Bottomley's portrayal of gradual deterioration of language in his poem 'Babel: The Gate of the God' (*Chambers of Imagery* II, 1912): 'Birds molten, touchly talc veins bronze buds crumble/ Ablid ublai ghan isz rad eighar ghaurl...' and to de la Mare's *The Listeners*. Some poems in *The Poetical Works of Wilfrid Scawen Blunt*, mentioned in the letter to Hudson, bear comparison with Thomas's work. The image of a 'roundelay' of a 'choir of thrushes' in Blunt's 'A Day in Sussex' is echoed in Thomas's 'Home [2]','March' and 'The Thrush'. Blunt's 'Ambition' starts and ends in a similar way to Thomas's 'Ambition'.

'**October**': Compare the opening lines of 'October' with the first lines of Robert Bridges's 'North Wind in October' (1894): 'In the golden glade the chestnuts are fallen all; / From the sered boughs of the oak the acorns fall'. In a 16 February 1913 letter to Hudson, Thomas calls Bridges 'a very perfect poet'; he refers to Bridges's 'loveliness, his purity and his originality' in a March 1913 *Bookman* review of *The Poetical Works of Robert Bridges*. He reviewed this book again in *The Daily Chronicle* in July 1913, and in August 1913 writes to Hudson, 'I would as soon read his best lyrics as Campion's'. In the second letter to Farjeon, Bertie is Farjeon's brother.

'This is no case of petty right or wrong': In the letter to Frost, Thomas refers to the literary editor J.C. Squire; John Masefield; T.E. Hulme; Wyndham Lewis's short-lived Vorticist journal *Blast*; Austin Harrison, editor of *The Observer* and *English Review*; and Chandler, the Ledington farmer with whom Thomas and his family stayed in August 1914. The Defence of the Realm Act (August 1914) gave the government powers to suppress published criticism without debate, to imprison without trial and to commandeer economic resources for the war effort.

1916

'Roads': See also de la Mare's 'Evening', *Poems* (1906). In the letter to Bottomley, Thomas mentions the artist James Guthrie, who illustrated some of his poems and published six in a booklet, *Six Poems by Edward Eastaway* (1916).

The Household Poems: The reference to Davies in the letter to Bottomley of 24 April 1916 alludes to a series of public poetry readings.

'If I Should Ever by Chance': Compare also Thomas's itemisation of plants in 'Adlestrop' with similar lists in de la Mare's 'The Hawthorn hath a deathly smell' (*The Listeners*, 1912), and 'A Widow's Weeds' (*Peacock Pie*, 1913). Both these poems were anthologised by Thomas in *Flowers I love* (1916), while de la Mare quoted 'Adlestrop' in its entirety in his 18 October 1917 *Times Literary Supplement* review of Thomas's *Poems*, and included it in his 1928 anthology *Come Hither*.

'What Shall I Give': See Eleanor Farjeon's 'King's Cross' and 'Bishopsgate' in the March and April 1916 issue of *Punch* and in *Nursery Rhymes of London Town* (1916).

'Some eyes condemn': In the letter to Eleanor Farjeon, 'autobiography' refers to *The Childhood of Edward Thomas*.

'The sun used to shine': In the 19 September 1914 letter to Frost, the two articles are 'This England' and 'Tipperary', the autobiography is *The Childhood of Edward Thomas*, and 'Harriet' is Harriet Monroe, editor of *Poetry*.

'No One Cares Less than I': On 20 May 1916 Thomas saw a performance of Rupert Brooke's 'Lithuania', writing critically of it to Frost the next day as 'only painting with Russian paints'. Only this extract from the letter to Haines is extant.

'Early One Morning': The Farjeon letter refers to her three-year-old niece.

'The Green Roads': The letter to de la Mare refers to Clifford Bax and

Ralph Hodgson, writers and friends of Thomas. 'Miss Loo' and 'The Three Cherry Trees' are poems in de la Mare's *The Listeners* (1912). De la Mare had a free life subscription to the London Library, which he shared with Thomas. 'Dick' is one of de la Mare's sons.

'**The Swifts**': See note on 'Haymaking', p. 192 above, for possible origins of the bow image.

'**Blenheim Oranges**': R.G. Thomas dates this poem from 3 September 1916, but in a letter to Eleanor Farjeon of 27 August 1916 Thomas writes 'I got tired of logarithms and wrote 8 verses which you see before you.'

'**The Trumpet**': In the 25 September 1916 letter to Farjeon, Bertie is her brother.

'**The long small room**': In the second letter to Farjeon 'the book' is her *Nursery Rhymes of London Town* (1916).

'**The Sheiling**': 'Morris' in the letter to Bottomley is a review book of Thomas's. The anthology is Thomas's *This England*.

'**Out in the dark**': See also the last four verses of de la Mare's 'The Dwelling-Place' (pp. 144–5), his 'The Lamplighter' in *Songs of Childhood* (1902), and 'Reverie' and 'Fear' in *Poems* (1906). De la Mare anthologised 'Out in the dark' in *Come Hither* (1928). See also Thomas Hardy's 'The Fallow Deer at the Lonely House' in *Late Lyrics and Earlier* (1922).

Select Bibliography

For details of unpublished manuscripts and documents see A Note on the Texts, p. xxvii.

Works and anthologies by Edward Thomas

Beautiful Wales (London: Black, 1905)

The Pocket Book of Songs and Poems for the Open Air (London: E. Grant Richards, 1907)

Light and Twilight (London: Duckworth, 1911)

Selected Poems of Edward Thomas, introduction by Edward Garnett (Newtown: Gregynog Press, 1927)

Poems and Last Poems, ed. Edna Longley (London: Collins, 1973)

The Collected Poems of Edward Thomas, ed. R.G. Thomas (Oxford: Oxford University Press, 1978)

A Language Not to Be Betrayed: Selected Prose of Edward Thomas, ed. Edna Longley (Manchester: Carcanet Press, 1981)

Edward Thomas on the Georgians, ed. Richard Emeny (Cheltenham: Cyder Press, 2004)

'Birds in March', *Edward Thomas Fellowship Newsletter*, 53 (January 2005), 11–13

Reviews and articles by Thomas appeared in pre-1917 issues of *The Academy, The Bookman, The Daily Chronicle, The Daily News, The English Review, The Morning Post, The Nation, The New Weekly, Poetry and Drama, Saturday Review* and *T.P.'s Weekly*

Correspondence of Edward Thomas

'Edward Thomas's Letters to W.H. Hudson', ed. James Guthrie, *The London Mercury* II.10 (August 1920), 434-42

Edward Thomas: The Last Four Years, Eleanor Farjeon (Oxford: Oxford University Press, 1958)

Letters from Edward Thomas to Gordon Bottomley, ed. R.G. Thomas (London: Oxford University Press, 1968)

Edward Thomas: A Selection of Letters to Edward Garnett, ed. Edward Garnett (Edinburgh: Tragara Press, 1981)

Edward Thomas's Letters to Jesse Berridge, ed. Anthony Berridge (London: Enitharmon, 1983)

Edward Thomas: Selected Letters, ed. R.G. Thomas (Oxford: Oxford University Press, 1995)

Letters to Helen, ed. R.G. Thomas (Manchester: Carcanet Press, 2000)

The Life and Letters of Edward Thomas, by John C. Moore (London: Heinemann, 1939)

Elected Friends: Robert Frost and Edward Thomas to One Another, ed. Matthew Spencer (New York: Handsel Books, 2003)

'To John Freeman', *Edward Thomas Fellowship Newsletter*, 32 (February 1995), 12–13

'The Letters of Edward Thomas to John Freeman', *Edward Thomas Fellowship Newsletter*, 38 (January 1998), 3–17

'Letters to Garnett and Hudson', *Edward Thomas Fellowship Newsletter*, 52 (August 2004), 6–17

'Letters to Gordon Bottomley', *Edward Thomas Fellowship Newsletter*, 55 (January 2006), 10–18

Related Works

Emeny, Richard, ed., *Edward Thomas 1878–1917: Towards a Complete Checklist of his Publications* (Blackburn: White Sheep Press, 2004)

Thomas, Myfanwy, *One of These Fine Days: Memoirs* (Manchester: Carcanet Press, 1982)

Whistler, Theresa, *Imagination of the Heart: The Life of Walter de la Mare* (London: Duckworth, 1993)

Books by Thomas's contemporaries

Abercrombie, Lascelles, *Interludes and Poems* (London: John Lane, 1908)

Lyrics and Unfinished Poems (Newtown: Gregynog Press, 1940)

Blunt, Wilfrid, *The Poetical Works of Wilfrid Scawen Blunt* (London: Macmillan, 1914)

Bottomley, Gordon, *Chambers of Imagery* II (London: Elkin Mathews, 1912)

Poems of Thirty Years (London: Constable, 1925)

Poems and Plays (London: Bodley Head, 1953)

Bridges, Robert, *Poetical Works of Robert Bridges* (London: Oxford University Press, 1912)

Davies, W.H., *Songs of Joy and Others* (London, A.C. Fifield, 1911)

Foliage: Various Poems (London: Elkin Mathews, 1913; repr. Cape, 1922)

Davies, William, Vivian Locke Ellis and James Guthrie, *In Memoriam: Edward Thomas* (London: Morland Press, 1919)

De la Mare, Walter, *The Collected Poems of Walter de la Mare* (London: Faber and Faber, 1979)

Fairless, Michael [pseud. Margaret Fairless Barber], *The Roadmender* (London: Duckworth, 1915)

Farjeon, Eleanor, *Dream-Songs for the Beloved* (London: Orpheus Press, the Orpheus Series, 5, Spring 1911)

Nursery Rhymes of London Town (London: Duckworth, 1916)

Freeman, John, *Collected Poems* (London: Macmillan, 1928)

Frost, Robert, *North of Boston* (London: Nutt, 1914)

Mountain Interval (New York: Henry Holt, 1916)

Hardy, Thomas, *The Complete Poems of Thomas Hardy*, ed. James Gibson (London: Macmillan, 1971)

Hudson, W.H., *The Land's End* (London: Hutchinson, 1908)

Dead Man's Plack, An Old Thorn and Poems (London: Dent, 1924)

Moore, T. Sturge, *The Little School: A Posy of Poems.* (London: Eragny Press, 1905)

Young, Geoffrey Winthrop, *Wind and Hill Poems* (London: Smith, Elder, 1909)

Freedom: Poems (London: Smith, Elder, 1914)

Further Reading

Works and anthologies by Edward Thomas

Horae Solitariae (London: Duckworth, 1902)

Rose Acre Papers, (London: S.C. Brown, 1904)

The South Country (London: Dent, 1909)

Rest and Unrest (London: Duckworth (1910)

Feminine Influence on the Poets (London: Martin Secker, 1910)

Walter Pater (London: Martin Secker, 1913)

The Happy-go-lucky Morgans (London: Duckworth, 1913)

This England: An Anthology from her Writers (London: Oxford University Press, 1915)

Four-and-Twenty Blackbirds (London: Duckworth, 1915)

The Flowers I Love (London: Jack, 1916)

Keats (London: Jack, 1916)

The Last Sheaf (London: Jonathan Cape, 1928)

The Childhood of Edward Thomas: A Fragment of Autobiography (London: Faber and Faber, 1938)

Edward Thomas on Thomas Hardy, ed. by Trevor Johnson (Cheltenham: Cyder Press, 2002)

Books by Thomas's contemporaries

Bottomley, Gordon, *King's Lear's Wife and Other Plays* (London: Constable, 1920)

Davies, W.H., *New Poems* (London: Elkin Mathews, 1907)

De la Mare, Walter, *The Riddle and other stories* (London: Selwyn and Blount, 1923)

Farjeon, Eleanor, *Trees* (London: Batsford, 1914)

    A Sussex Alphabet (Bognor Regis: Pear Tree Press, 1939)

Frost, Robert, *A Boy's Will* (London: Nutt, 1913)

    West-Running Brook (New York: Henry Holt, 1928; written in 1914)

    As Told to a Child (Cheltenham: Cyder Press, 2000)

Hudson, W.H., *Adventures Among Birds* (London: Hutchinson, 1913)

    Green Mansions: A Romance of the Tropical Forest (London: Duckworth, 1904, repr. 1911)

Related reading

Eckert, Robert, *Edward Thomas: A Biography and a Bibliography* (London: Dent, 1937)

Francis, Lesley Lee, *The Frost Family's Adventure in Poetry* (Columbia: University of Missouri Press, 1994)

Harvey, Anne, ed., *Elected Friends: Poems for and about Edward Thomas* (London: Enitharmon, 1991)

Longley, Edna, *Poetry in the Wars* (Newcastle: Bloodaxe, 1986)

Mertins, Louis, *Robert Frost: Life and Talks-Walking* (Norman: University of Oklahoma, 1966)

Thomas, R.G., *Edward Thomas: A Portrait* (Oxford: Clarendon Press, 1985)

Related Journals and Newspapers

Bottomley, Gordon, 'A Note on Edward Thomas', *Welsh Review*, 4.3 (September 1945), 166-76

Georgian Poetry 1911–1912, ed. Edward Marsh (London: Poetry Bookshop, 1912)

Georgian Poetry 1913–1915, ed. Edward Marsh (London: Poetry Bookshop, 1915)

Kendall, Judy, 'The Dating of Edward Thomas's Mature Verse', *Notes and Queries* (September 2006), 346–7

Index of Names, Letters and Works

Edward Thomas's Poets

the Trees' 78; 'The Tuft of Flowers' 32, 177; 'The Wood Pile' 32, 57–8

Galsworthy, John xiv
Garnett, Edward xiv, 85, 97, 181, 186–7; **Letters** xxii, 16–17, 31–2, 35–7, 43, 64–5, 173–4, 189n, 190n, 192n; **Works** *An Imaged World: Poems in Prose* 187; 'Spring in a London Square' 187
Georgian Poetry anthology series 42, 162, 189n
Gibson, Wilfrid 178
Goethe, Johann Wolfgang von 128
Gray, Thomas 173
Gunn, Neil Miller 92
Guthrie, James 107, 134, 140, 161, 193n

Haines, J.W. xiv, xxi, 54, 64–5, 69, 70, 71, 138, 178, 180, 187; **Letters** xxi, xxv, 47–9, 136, 179–82, 193n; **Work** 'Edward Thomas' xviii
Hardy, Thomas **Works** 'The Caged Thrush Freed and Home Again' 191n; 'The Darkling Thrush' 191n; 'The Fallow Deer at the Lonely House' 194n; 'Men Who March Away' 85–6; 'On Sturminster Foot-Bridge' 192n; 'The Pine Planters' 192n; 'The Spring Call' 191n
Harrison, Austin 97, 193n
Heinemann, W.H. 22, 190n
Hodgson, Ralph xiv, 59, 145, 162, 191n, 193n
Housman, A.E. **Work** 'Reveille' 192n
Hudson, W.H. xiii, xiv, 172, 176, 181, 187–8, 192n; **Letters** xiv, xvii, xx, xxv, 16–18, 48, 85–6, 187, 189n, 192–3n; **Works** *Adventures Among Birds* 187; *Afoot in England* 187; *Green Mansions* 187; *Hampshire Days* 187; 'In the Wilderness' 15, *The Land's End* 47–8; 'The London

Sparrow' 103; *A Shepherd's Life* 187
Hulme, T.E. 97, 193n

Ingpen, Roger 157, 171, 172

Jefferies, Richard **Works** *The Amateur Poacher* 192n; *The Scarlet Shawl* 172
John, Edmund 122
Jung, Carl, 191n

Keats, John 46, 52–3, 191n

Lewis, Wyndham 193n
Louis XIII **Works** 'Amaryllis' 39; 'Orientis Partibus adventavit asinus' 39

Mabinogion 181
MacAlister, Ian **Letter** xiv
Marsh, Edward 5, 189n
Masefield, John 97, 193n
Meredith, George 86
Meynell, Alice 125
Meynell, Viola 9, 189n
Milton, John 127
Monro, Harold xxii, 5, 22, 37, 58–60, 80, 114, 189n
Monroe, Harriet 135, 193n
Moore, T. Sturge 69–72; **Work** 'Lubber Breeze' 191n
Morris, William 105, 161, 187, 194n

Nash, Paul 110, 122
New Numbers 178
Newbolt, Henry xiii, 114
Noble, James Ashcroft 184

Pater, Walter xvi, 171, 172–3, 175, 176
Plato 128–9, 183
Prior, Matthew 61

Radford, Maitland 9, 157, 189n
Raleigh, Walter 44
Ransome, Arthur xiii, 72
Rawnsley, Canon Hardwicke 83, 192n

Edward Thomas's Poets

Reynolds, Stephen xiii
Richards, Grant xix
Roberts, Morley 188
Rossetti, Dante Gabriel 128, 183
Ruskin, John 137

Saintsbury, George 145
Scott-James R.A. xiii, 37, 55, 59, 191n
Seccombe, Thomas xiii
Shakespeare, William 20, 72, 128; **Work** *Sonnets* 61, 128
Shaw, G.B. 184
Shelley, P.B. 138; **Works** *Adonais* 44; 'The Sensitive Plant' 17, 189n
Smith, J.C. 178
Spenser, Edmund **Work** *The Fairie Queene* 178
Squire, Jack Collings 97, 193n
Swinburne, A.C. xvi, 171, 185; **Works** 'A Ballad of Life' 85; 'In the Orchard' 85; 'Itylus' 85

Tchaikovsky, Pyotr Ilyich 88
Tennyson, Alfred 86, 127
Thomas, Bronwen xxiv, 40, 55, 88, 97, 115–16, 135, 148–9, 155, 167, 176–7, 191n
Thomas, Edward **Letters** passim; **Poems** 'Adlestrop' 193n; 'After Rain' xxii, 8–9, 17, 122, 189n; 'After you speak' 181; 'Ambition' 192n; *An Annual of New Poetry* 111, 122, 182, 184; 'An Old Song [I]' ('I was not apprenticed nor ever dwelt in famous Lincolnshire') 8; 'And You, Helen' 121, 122; 'April' 37, 54, 191n; 'The Ash Grove' 182; 'Aspens' xviii, 77, 79, 81, 122, 192n; 'The Barn and the Down' xxii, 44; 'Beauty' 17; 'Blenheim Oranges' 150–1, 194n; 'Bob's Lane' ('Women he loved') 141; 'But these things also' 31, 190n; 'Celandine' 110; 'The Child in the Orchard' 154–5; 'The Child on the Cliff' 29–30, 190n; 'The clouds that are so light' 99–100;

'Cock-Crow' xxii, 84–5, 192n; 'Cuckoo' 31; 'Digging [1]' ('Today I think') 46–7, 191n; 'Digging [2]' ('What matter makes my spade for tears or mirth?') 82–3, 192n; 'A Dream' xxii, 75–6; 'Early One Morning' 139–40, 193n; 'Eluned' xiv, 39, 67–8, 190n; 'Fifty Faggots' 57–60, 62, 180–1, 191n; 'The Glory' 122; 'Go now' ('Like the Touch of Rain') xviii, 124–5; 'Goodnight' 31; 'The Green Roads' 141, 143, 146, 193–4n; 'Haymaking' 73–4, 192n, 194n; 'Home' 109–10; 'Home [2]' ('Often I had gone this way before') xxiv, 50, 52, 191n, 192n; 'Household Poems' 116, 118, 122, 193; 'I built myself a house of glass' 64, 178, 191–2n; 'If I Should Ever by Chance' 115–16, 122, 193n; 'If I were to Own' 117–18, 122; 'Interval' 11–12, 189n; 'It Rains' 124; 'It was upon' 141; 'Lights Out' 154–5, 156–7, 159; 'Lob' xvi, xxii, xxiii, 35, 36, 41–4, 54, 59, 69, 92, 107, 190–91n; 'The Lofty Sky' 24–5, 190n; 'The long small room' xxii, 75, 158–9, 194n; 'The Manor Farm' 16–18, 189n; 'March' 6–7; 'The Mountain Chapel' 14–15, 189n; 'The New House' 19, 33, 160, 190n; 'No One Cares Less than I' 136, 193n; 'November' 3–4, 17, 189n; 'October' xvi, 87–9, 192–3n; 'Old Man' 31; 'The Owl' 27–8; 'Out in the Dark' 143, 163–7, 194n; 'Over The Hills' 192n; *Poems* (1917) 118, 186; 'The Pond' ('Bright Clouds') 15; 'Rain' 106, 107, 113; 'Roads' 101–4, 106–8, 181, 193n; 'Sedge-Warblers' 62–3; 'The Sheiling' 160, 184, 194n; 'The Signpost' 17, 31; *Six Poems* 107, 193n; 'Snow' xxiv, 21–2, 190n; 'Some eyes condemn' 127,

Index of the Creative Process

covering introductory texts, letters and footnotes but not the content of poems

63, 138, 161, 174, 175, 177, 184
Intention, *see* effort
Intuition, *see* instinct

Japanese influence 159

Last lines xxii, 17, 75–6, 93, 159
Leisure, *see* boredom
Letters as poems xv–xvi, 87
Line divisions, lengths and endings
xxiv, 12, 36, 63, 88, 127–8, 129,
153
Lists 115, 118, 193n
Lyric, short poems xiv, xxii, 112,
178

Memories 9, 30, 52, 171, 177
Mundane incidents xxii, 31, 84
Myth, legend xvi, 84–6, 184;
British 161; Celtic xvi; Norse
xvi, 20, 183, 190n; Welsh 107,
181

Names xxi, 16, 40, 86, 88, 107,
115, 116
Narrative poem, *see* epic
Notebook dependency xviii
Nouns 85, 105
Nursery rhymes xxiv, 23

Oral tradition xxiii–xxiv

Perfection xxiv, 4, 9, 28, 32, 43, 46,
57, 86, 105, 128, 192n
Periphrasis, *see* divagations
Plagiarism 129
Plainness, homeliness, simplicity
xxii, 22, 28, 56, 68, 72, 76, 85,
105, 137, 166, 173–4, 184, 191n
Poetry's relation to prose xvi, xvii,
xxii, 4, 9, 27–8, 36, 59–60, 62,
72, 90–2, 117–18, 125, 133,
134–5, 175, 177, 178
Precision, *see* exactness
Prose poems xiv, xvii, 178, 187
Proverbs and mottoes xxiii, 22, 23,
36, 64, 74, 90, 92, 117–18, 185
Publication of poems xv, 18, 26,
59, 60, 107–8, 114, 122, 157,
180, 182, 184

Publication of prose xv, 22, 70
Punctuation and capitalisation xv,
xxiii, 23, 107, 138, 153

Reading, misreading xxii, xxiv, 36,
61, 80–1, 86, 145–7, 148–9,
158, 159, 169, 175, 178–9
Repetition 47, 60, 151
Restlessness 110, 112
Reviewers, criticism of poetry 17,
32, 44, 55–6, 59–60, 69–72, 80,
105–6, 107–8, 112, 127–9, 136–
8, 145–7, 159, 166, 172, 173–4,
179–80, 184–7
Revision xviii, xx, xxii, 4, 9, 17, 35–
6, 37, 44, 72, 83, 89, 91, 92, 93,
98, 106–7, 140, 149, 158–9
Rhetoric 9, 128, 176
Rhyme xxii, xxiv, 4–5, 9, 23, 36,
63, 80, 82–3, 87, 88, 115, 116,
117, 127, 164, 165, 174–5, 179,
185, 189n
Rhythm and metre xxi, xxii, xxiii,
xxiv, 5, 9, 13, 17, 23, 35–6, 37,
56, 59–60, 68, 88, 119, 137,
179, 183, 185, 191n

Scent 46–8
Secrecy in composing 90–1, 153
Self-consciousness xviii, xix, xx,
xxi, 64–5, 171, 173, 175, 177
Self-expression 32, 63, 103, 129,
137–8, 179
Short poems, *see* lyric
Sickness, *see* injury
Simplicity, *see* plainness
Simultaneous conception and
execution, spontaneity 58, 60,
79–80, 175, 176, 179
Song and music xiv, xix, xxiv, 9,
39, 40, 48, 61, 115, 139–40,
151, 152–3, 184, 189n;
'Greensleeves' 39; 'John Peel'
xxiv; 'Mr McKinley' 158; 'Pleur
du cerf' 20, 'Rio Grande' 39,
139–40
Sonnets 61, 83, 127–9, 136, 137,
141
Sound xxiii, xxiv, 36, 47, 55,
128–9

Edward Thomas's Poets